Limitless Real Estate Strategies

Build Your Wealth and Join The Real Estate Revolution

STEVE D. VALENTINE

Limitless Real Estate Strategies
Build Your Wealth and Join the Real Estate Revolution

Copyright © 2023 Reflek Publishing
All rights reserved.

No part of this publication may be reproduced, distributed, or transmitted in any form or by any means, including photocopying, recording, or other electronic or mechanical methods, without the prior written permission of the publisher, except in the case of brief quotations embodied in critical reviews and certain other noncommercial uses permitted by copyright law.

Disclaimer: The author makes no guarantees concerning the level of success you may experience by following the advice and strategies contained in this book, and you accept the risk that results will differ for each individual. The purpose of this book is to educate, entertain, and inspire.

For more information: hello@stevedvalentine.com

ISBN: 978-1-7378283-4-1 (print)
ISBN: 978-1-7378283-3-4 (e-book)

I wrote this for you: the real estate professional who needs to break free from the norm.

You have LIMITLESS potential to build the real estate business and investment portfolio you desire, the wealth that will create the life you love, and the legacy you want to leave behind.

Get ready to go rogue to make it happen!

HERE'S A GIFT
BEFORE YOU EVEN BEGIN!

To say thanks for buying this book, here's a bonus gift to help you take action today! - Steve

Get your free gifts here:

www.stevedvalentine.com/bookresources

Praise for
Limitless Real Estate Strategies

"Steve is a trustworthy source in an industry that can lack trust. He is a wealth of specialized knowledge and has helped me, my agents, and even some of my clients when his specialty was needed."

—*Brian North - Owner North & Co*

"So Much Knowledge! The experience that Steve brings to the table and the knowledge he has in every aspect of the Real Estate industry is exceptional! He freely shares it to help others learn and grow and become better every day!"

—*Wende Valentine - Owner BLR construction*

"I have a number of properties that I currently own and a few more in the process of being purchased using knowledge and lessons from Steve."

—*Andrew Monohan - Agent*

"Steve is THE reason my husband Seena and I got into real estate investing and it has completely changed the trajectory of our entire life. I truly mean this. Prior to meeting Steve, I had a thriving business but it required ME to be on all the time. He taught us how to think about LEGACY, impact and wealth in a very different lineage changing way. What he taught us about real estate, creative financing and generating wealth helped us strategically scale from ZERO DOLLARS in real estate to owning 4 investment properties worth 3.5 million in 13 months. I truly cannot even IMAGINE what our business, let alone LIFE would be like without Steve; one of my FAVORITE humans on the planet."

—Seena and Kacia Ghetmiri

"Steve is a master at problem-solving and creating win/wins for all parties involved. His ability to quickly think outside of the box, articulate a plan, and get everyone comfortable is his genius. It is unparalleled."

—Marshall Morris

"Steve's maverick spirit comes through in his approach to real estate. For too long successful real estate investors and agents have kept the secrets of the trade close to their vest. Steve shares with a limitless mindset!"

—George Laughton - CEO Laughton Team

"I have seen Steve grow over the years from being a client with many questions to now as a business partner with incredible knowledge, work ethic, integrity and unbelievable concern to help others grow in their financial success!"

—Howard Weiner

"Steve changed my life! He showed me creative ways of looking at real estate and building wealth. Steve has the most incredible ability to get to know your goals and connect you with creative solutions. He is unselfish and truly cares for all his clients. So grateful for his friendship and partnership."

—*Elliot Schwartz*

"The most thoughtful, creative, investor I know. He has an endless tool belt of options to solve problems."

—*Templton Walker*

"Steve is truly a LIMITLESS thinker and creator when it comes to Real Estate!! He's the best in the industry. Period. He can put ANY deal together and make ANY real estate scenario a WIN-WIN for EVERYONE involved!!! It's amazing to watch!!!!"

—*Dan & Megan Valentine*

"Steve did a course that spanned over several weeks called Limitless that my husband and I participated in. I would have considered us fairly savvy investors and as a 20-year real estate broker myself I didn't realize how much there was still left to learn but Steve shared several valuable strategies that we still use to this day."

—*Carin Nguyen – Real Estate Agent & Team Owner Carin Nguyen and Bestselling Author*

"Steve has the ability to problem solve and find solutions where impossible seems to be the starting point. The wisdom in this book can help you go from zero to hero and build and investment portfolio that you never thought possible.

Steve has multiple decades of experience in the real estate industry. In fact, he cut his teeth knowing how to

build solutions for people. His mind, his heart, and his drive are all founded in helping others."
— *Kimberly Ryan – Real Brokerage AZ Growth Leader*

Contents

Introduction 1
1. Good Agents Are Made in Tough Markets 10
2. Five Myths We Need to Bust 23
3. From Agent to Problem Solver 38
4. The Problem-Solver's Mindset 44
5. The Limitless Strategy Tool Box 59
Make a Lasting Impact in Real Time 74
6. People Over Profit 76
7. Let Your Clients Choose Their Own Adventure 84
8. Be Prepared to Pivot 92
9. Invest In Yourself 99
10. Limitless Real Estate Strategies 111
Here's What to Do Next 136
Acknowledgments 139
About the Author 143

Introduction

Your real estate license is a powerful thing, more powerful than you may realize. It's the key to the door of opportunity—a tool you can use to create wealth that you can pass down for generations. *And it works in any market.*

Inside this book is everything you need to know to start building your wealth today. In these pages, I share the same strategies I used to rebuild my life from financial ruin after the US financial crisis of 2007 and 2008 to the eight-figure portfolio of 86 properties (and counting) I own today. By the end of this book, you'll have the knowledge and the mindset to create your own legacy of wealth. All you have to do is learn to look beyond the next commission.

As you go through this book, there will be tons of resources and videos to help you take the concepts from this book and apply them on your journey to building wealth. You can get access to all of this for free at www.Stevedvalentine.com/bookresources.

As a coach, mentor, podcaster, and owner of two multimillion- dollar businesses, I teach Realtors, and my own clients, how to become investors and build a financial legacy using creative outside-the-box thinking to solve any real estate problem. *Real estate is not just a business of selling other people's houses.* Agents have multiple income streams available to them, but nobody in the industry is talking about all the options. That's why I wrote this book.

First, there's traditional commission-based sales. Most agents focus their entire careers on earning money this way. Secondly there is wholesaling, when agents, and non-agents, who are good at finding deals flip real estate contracts for a fee. My favorite, of course, is real estate investing, which can consist of your typical fix-and-flip houses or houses that you buy as a source of rental income—either from tenants or as short-term vacation rental properties.

Investing is how you create a legacy, and it's what we focus on in this book using real properties instead of stocks, bonds, and traditional retirement accounts. Once you become an expert in real estate investing, you can work with investor clients *and* become an investor yourself. Not one or the other, but simultaneously.

What I want you to understand is you can wrap up all these income streams into your day-to-day business and build your own wealth alongside the wealth you help your clients build.

Before we get started, let's acknowledge how overused the word "investor" is. From the perspective of someone outside the industry, when a consumer hears a real estate agent use that word, they immediately think they're about to get screwed by a low baller looking for a deal or a big corporation that wants to destroy houses to build something else. Instead of just calling myself an "investor," I use the term "problem solver." I use the two terms interchangeably

INTRODUCTION

throughout this book. Think of it like this: I'm teaching you to invest in real estate by solving someone else's problem.

Every time I approach a new client, I go into the conversation with this question:

> "What is the problem I need to solve?"

This is how I make each experience a win-win for me and my clients.

So let me ask you:

If you could get a 50% return on your money every year by investing in real estate, would you do it?

Say you have $300,000 you want to invest. Obviously, you're looking for the highest return you can get from that money without risking it all, right? Let's say you decide to buy Tesla stock or something else on the stock market. The first year, you earn 10% interest, the next year it drops to five, then it goes back up a little, and so on. If you were unlucky enough to buy Enron stocks, your investment is now zero.

Let's look at what happens to your money when you invest in real estate instead. Say you buy a house worth $300,000 — still a median house price in many parts of the US. You put $9,000 down, and the house appreciates $18,000 in the first year. You've earned *100% interest* on your investment in a single year, and you only had to invest $9,000 of your own money. Even if your house doesn't appreciate that first year, you still own an asset that's worth $300,000. In the stock market, you have to come up with $300,000 of *your own money* to create an asset of the same value.

So now you've bought a $300,000 investment with only a fraction of the cash up front compared to the stock market option. You've also bought future down payments on more houses because you can turn around and use the equity in

that first house to repeat this process again and again. As your equity grows over time, you will have increasingly more cash available to pull out of each house you buy. Yes, you have a mortgage, or other debt you used to buy the house, but as you will learn in this book, you can set up your portfolio so the rental income covers all, or most, of the cost of owning each house. You may have some negative cash flow at different times throughout your investment. Depending on your particular goals, long-term strategy, and circumstances, the cash flow will eventually become a very generous income.

You can't rent out your stock portfolio.

Over a thirty-year timeframe, if you look at the average rate of return on the stock market compared to the average appreciation of real estate, the latter almost always fares better. Aside from that, with real estate, you can grow your money exponentially faster. Why? Because you don't need as much money upfront to buy property.

How long would it take you to save $300,000 to buy Tesla stock? How long would it take you to save $9,000 to buy a house? Totally different scenarios, right?

Here's where real estate investing gets even more powerful. After a year or two of owning your home, which has now appreciated by $18,000, I would advise you to refinance and

INTRODUCTION

pull out some of that equity to buy a second rental house. Now you own two houses! You doubled your net worth in a relatively short amount of time, *for the same initial investment of $9,000 of your own cash*. Rental income covers most of the ownership costs, your first house bought the down payment on the second, and you now have two houses from which to pull equity to buy house number three in another twelve months or so. Yes, your mortgage payment went up. So did market rents that pay those mortgages. Repeat that over twenty or thirty years and you'll have a portfolio potentially worth tens of millions of dollars.

Even if the real estate market slumps and those houses don't appreciate every single year, you still own those assets. When the stock market slumps, you could lose your entire life's savings overnight. You have nothing but a bunch of hypothetical numbers sitting in accounts to show for all that money you invested. Real estate is a physical asset that will always retain its value long-term. Your original investment is protected, and you can access it at any time, if you need to.

Do you see how powerful this is? If you want to dive deeper into this concept, visit www.Stevedvalentine.com/bookresources for more info.

Some of you may fear the current market. As I write this, it's early 2023, and the market is volatile as interest rates climb to fight inflation. This is *not* the time to cry, *"The sky is falling!"* and wait for the market to boom again before you start to buy.

A tough market is a prime opportunity zone for an investor/problem solver!

If I'd had that mindset in 2008, I would have saved myself from extreme financial hardship sooner and had a vastly larger net worth today.

Let's look at the key benefits of investing and all the ways that owning real estate can change your financial future. To do this, I like to have my coaching clients do a fun exercise to unlock the possibilities. I call it the "Wouldn't It Be Cool If" game. I want you to do this exercise now—just write down your answers to that question.

For you, maybe this looks like the following:

- Wouldn't it be cool if I could pay for my child's college education with cash?
- Wouldn't it be cool if I were in the position to take care of my parents when they retire?
- Wouldn't it be cool if I had $10,000 a month in passive income? Or $20,000? How about $50,000?
- Wouldn't it be cool if I could own $5,000,000 worth of rental properties by the time I reach age forty?

This exercise gives you permission to dream about what life could look like ten or twenty years down the road. These dreams become your goals as an investor. Throughout this book, I'm going to show you how to start with your goals and reverse engineer a plan to get there. Your dreams and goals will motivate you to carry out your plan.

INTRODUCTION

My mentor, my dad, was a brilliant real estate strategist who helped build mountains of wealth for his many investor clients. *He never used any of that ingenuity for himself.* When he died of cancer in 2015, he left behind a very small insurance policy, lots of debt, and only one property he owned. While he left our family with a mountain of debt, he also left me with a mountain of knowledge of things I can do, and things I *shouldn't* do, which has led me down the road of educating the industry and my clients how to build wealth over time through real estate.

I wrote this book to make sure what happened to my dad never happens to you, your clients, or anyone else in this industry.

Once you understand the power of real estate investing, it's easy to guide your clients to the same life you desire, and it's why I founded my coaching platform at www.SteveDValentine.com, where I teach situational awareness in real estate, coach private clients, and build wealth strategies for my clients through real estate. Some of my coaching clients have increased their net worth by more than a million dollars in less than six months by following the strategies I share in this book. I hope you'll take what you learn from these pages and spread this knowledge even further.

This book shows you how to work as hard for yourself as you do for your clients. I've condensed everything I've learned from building my own eight-figure portfolio (and coaching hundreds of other agents to do the same) into a complete step-by-step guide that shows you how to build your own wealth *alongside* your clients.

I'll break down the biggest myths holding you back from building your own wealth and show you the key mindset shifts you need to make in order to prepare yourself for opportunities when they come your way—because opportunity already comes your way, all the time. You just need the insight to recognize it and the mindset to seize it. The definition of *luck* is when opportunity meets preparedness.

Through my signature Limitless Real Estate Strategy in Chapter 5, we'll look at your long-term financial goals and then reverse engineer your investment strategy to make sure your assets will provide the cash flow you need at the right times in your life—and a system setup to manage it all.

I'll also show you how to pay down debt quickly and create financial reserves so you can make your money work for you and be ready when opportunity comes knocking. By the end of this book, you'll have everything you need to put your entire plan in place and set it in motion.

Your greatest skill—and your key to success—is your ability to get to the bottom of what your clients need, to narrow down the best options, and then guide them as they choose the best solution.

When you go from agent to problem solver, you unlock the door to limitless opportunity—for yourself and your clients. You'll be able to pivot whenever you need to and make your money work for you, *no matter what the market is doing*. Instead of chasing the buyer and the commission, you will learn to chase the money and the opportunity.

INTRODUCTION

I'll show you my ten best investment strategies and share stories that illustrate their power. You'll learn creative solutions for many of the diverse real estate problems you'll encounter as you go forward in your career. Everything I share in this book you can implement today in your own business.

Along the way, you're going to learn how to help *a lot* of people. Because what I teach isn't about *selling*, it's about solving problems that help everyone involved—from your clients to your own family. A problem solver can build vast wealth for themselves and others, provide homes for people, and open doors for sellers whose complex problems nobody else could solve.

This is how you transform from a real estate agent locked in the limited mindset of a traditional agent, to a real estate strategist with limitless potential for business growth and personal wealth, in any market. You've already got the key to unlock it all—your real estate license. You just need the mindset and knowledge to find the right doors and turn the key.

This is a journey. If you're ready to stop selling and start solving, turn the page and let me show you how. If you want my personal guidance along the way, join my inner circle of others just like you at www.TheLimitlessCircle.com, or book a call with me by visiting www.SteveDValentine.com.

Let's build your legacy.

Steve Valentine

Chapter 1
Good Agents Are Made in Tough Markets

It wasn't until I lost almost everything that I was able to build the legacy of wealth that I have today. My greatest regret is that during the 2007–2008 market crash, I was so focused on figuring out how to create income that I missed the real opportunity right in front of me.

The 2008 financial crisis led me to working in the foreclosure space with Fannie Mae and Freddie Mac. What I didn't realize at the time was that the big money and opportunities for creating wealth was in buying the properties, not just working for a commission. Instead of raising capital and seeing all the opportunities, I was focused on digging myself out of the hole I created. I could have expedited that process if I had had the knowledge to invest, raise funds, and have investment conversations with clients. I could have created hundreds of millionaires (including myself), sent thousands of kids to college with no debt, and created a massive amount of wealth for my clients during this time had I just understood what was right in front of me.

My problem-solver mindset did not show up until my father passed in 2015. That's when I shifted my mindset from that of a traditional real estate agent focused on commissions, GCI (Gross Commission Income), and outperforming my competition, to the mindset of a problem solver who knows how to ask the right questions, get to the bottom of what my clients need, and find creative solutions with benefits that reach far beyond the sale.

Today, I teach other agents how to be creative, strategic, and *LIMITLESS*. My personal investment portfolio of 86 cash-flowing properties provides housing for dozens of families, all while building a financial legacy for my own family that will last for generations. In this book, I want to show you how far you can go if you stop thinking about the next commission and start solving problems for your clients.

I lost my father, Dan, to cancer just a few years after the US housing economy crash, yet all that adversity forced me to try new things. To take risks and say yes to opportunities first, and figure out how to make things work later. I discovered that my real estate license could open doors I'd never realized existed.

Good agents are made in tough markets.

I don't want it to be so hard for you. I can help you become one of the best agents in the industry and prevent you from having to fight your way through the kind of challenges I faced. I want you to achieve everything I did—and more, if that's what you want. My goal is for you to increase your net worth and your income by solving more problems for people.

Some of my coaching clients have increased their net worth by more than a million dollars in less than six months by buying multiple rental properties. Using the Buy Box method for discerning what makes the best rental property, which you'll learn about in Chapter 4, I've shown my coaching clients where to find those properties, how to finance the purchases, and how to structure everything so they can manage their portfolio.

First, I will tell you how I got from rock bottom to where I am today. In 2008, my parents' real estate company collapsed. At the time, Wende, and I were both employed in the family business and we had poured a million dollars of our own cash into the company—which also meant we were responsible for company loans that we had personally guaranteed. By the time we cut our losses and walked away from the business, we had one toddler and a baby, we were buried in debt, and we lost our own home to foreclosure.

You could say that my dad taught me almost everything I know about how to be a successful agent and investor. But not all of his lessons were good ones. Some of the best life lessons are the ones that teach you what *not* to do.

In the mid-1980s, my grandmother, who was one of the first female real estate brokers in Illinois, moved the family business to Arizona along with my parents, who were company partners with her. When I graduated from high school, my dad made sure I knew that if I ever wanted to learn the real estate business, the door was always open.

I'm a car guy, and back then, I wanted to work in the automotive industry. The last thing I wanted to do was run around all day showing houses like my parents did. Two years into my career as a mechanic, the contents of my toolbox were stolen. As much as I loved being a mechanic, I was tired of rolling around on the hot concrete in the summer, so I took it as an opportunity. I told my dad, "You know what? I can try the real estate thing." Which brings me to the first big lesson I learned from my dad.

Lesson #1: If you want luxuries, you have to work for them.

My dad was a good father with a generous spirit. He was also a creative problem solver, and he passed that ability on to me. He always taught me that I was going to have to work for the things I wanted. When I was twelve years old, I asked him to buy me a pair of $125 Air Jordan sneakers. Dad took me to Kmart and showed me the shoe rack. "As your father," he said, "the $15 tennis shoes on this rack are all I'm responsible for buying you. If you want the luxury of those Air Jordans, then, you're going to have to work for it."

I started doing odd jobs for my parents' company to earn that extra money for the Air Jordans. Eventually, I bought them. Years later, when I quite automotive and enrolled in real estate night school, I found myself back in that same position— earning extra income by working odd jobs for my parents during the day until I earned my license. True to his word, my dad welcomed me into the family business full-time.

If you are a new licensee, you need to be willing to learn from and listen to your mentors. My dad was instrumental in the way he taught me. Sitting at the edge of his desk listening to calls, I learned how to problem solve. At the time, I just didn't realize how much of a positive impact not receiving a commission check for the first two years in the business would make on me.

Lesson #2: Avoid the real estate roller coaster.

When I got into real estate, my dad wanted to make sure I didn't get on the real estate roller coaster. You know what I'm talking about, right? You work hard to sell a house, you get a big commission check, and then you stop putting in the work that it took you to get you there. And, because you suddenly have a big influx of cash, your spending habits increase. Eventually, you find yourself out of funds and right back where you started.

For the first two years, my dad made sure my job was more of an internship than a sales position. I didn't get any commission checks. I worked for $500 a week, plus some gas money and other paid expenses. Dad made me sit at the edge of his desk and listen to his phone conversations so I could understand the business from the perspective of an experienced professional, instead of trying to figure it out by my own trial and error. I spent a lot of time being mentored by both my parents, learning their processes and the creative problem solving that went into so many of the scenarios I watched them tackle.

Gradually, I started to work with buyers. I showed the houses and then sat with my dad while he negotiated the sales and wrote the contracts. My dad was very deliberate about the way he taught me about real estate, and I learned so much of what I call "situational awareness" from him (more on that in Chapter 3).

Lesson #3: It's not always a good idea to diversify your business.

In 2005, we were Realty Executives' #2 team, internationally. In that year alone, we sold around seven hundred properties to investors. That is when my dad started to take his eye off the ball.

"You know, I think we should start a painting company," he announced one day. "We already have a captured audience with our investment clients." Not long after, we opened a plumbing company, then carpentry, and so on until we owned six different construction entities. We were losing money in all of those side businesses, but the market was doing so well that the real estate side was making up for it. This is when we should have realized we needed to stay in our own lane, kept our head down and focused on what we were good at.

Then the market crashed in 2007. The business diversity my dad was so proud of caused the entire family company to collapse. Had we not become distracted by diversifying into construction companies in the previous two years, we probably could have salvaged enough to make it through the tough times together. Decisions continued to be made that I disagreed with, particularly with one investor who had lent us $175,000 as a second mortgage on the commercial building where we had our office. They offered to buy us out so they could get their money back, and we could just work from home. My dad refused to do it; my voice wasn't always heard.

I realized we needed to make a change, to separate ourselves from the situation. Wende and I made the decision, as a couple, to walk away from the family partnership. By this time, we had already put a $1,000,000 of our own cash into the business. We had also personally guaranteed the debt of a lot of those construction companies operating under the family business. We knew people had made individual loans to the company. They made them because they knew us and trusted us. We felt additional responsibility for those additional loans, personally, which totaled another $1,000,000.

Shortly after, we lost everything we owned and we were still left with debt. With the US economy in a crisis, nobody could sell anything on the market, so we had to abandon real estate altogether for a while. I started doing odd jobs, like sprinkler repairs, car repairs—anything I could do to survive. We were juggling our vehicles to hide them so they couldn't be repossessed by the bank.

As a man and father, one of my failing moments was watching my wife walk out the door to go wait tables. I thought, *after all the things we've done, Wende is going to wait tables because we're so broke.* My sense of failure was so profound, I actually wrote a suicide note.

On September 10, 2009, I received my big break with an opportunity to enter the foreclosure business. When we were given that opportunity in September of 2009, there were really only two types of real estate businesses thriving.

The first was short sales, where you're working with investor buyers; the second was what they call "real estate–owned accounts," or REOs, which were Fannie Mae and Freddie Mac mortgages. These were the foreclosure accounts. One day, my real estate broker called with what became the first "say yes and figure it out later" opportunity that changed the trajectory of my career and financial future.

"Hey, do you have ten thousand dollars?" she asked. "And do you want to work your ass off? Because I've got an opportunity that comes with a real estate account and a foreclosure account."

I immediately said yes. I didn't have $10,000. I didn't even know where I was going to get that kind of money. Since I believe in saying yes and figuring it out later, I told Wende, "We're going to have to put in twenty-hour days for who knows how long, but we're going to figure this out and raise $10,000 somehow."

Just two months into this big opportunity, I broke my neck doing an obstacle course. We spent Thanksgiving week in the hospital waiting for a surgery the doctor gave me a 50/50 shot of being paralyzed from. As a young married couple with two small boys, it was a lot to deal with in a very short period of time. Wende, and I agreed to keep my injury under wraps for fear of losing this opportunity. She and I worked tirelessly in the hospital to keep things moving. There I sat in a hospital bed and a neck brace, with a phone and laptop, pretending nothing had happened. This opportunity was going to be our shot, and I wasn't going to risk it for anything.

By the grace of God, we succeeded!

Back then, foreclosure accounts were huge, and we were able to carve out our space in that niche to become one of 40 or so agents in the area who were well known in the REO space. We worked harder than we ever had before and wound up turning that first account into a long-standing relationship that we did very well with for almost a decade.

By 2009, the banks were no longer taking on more REO agents; anyone trying to break into this niche was already too late to the game. For Wende and I, despite the weirdness of the market at that time, pivoting into foreclosure accounts allowed us to get back on our feet.

Over the next four years, we never filed bankruptcy. We paid off every penny of our debt and rebuilt our company. And by 2012, we were able to buy a new family home. We had been given the opportunity of a lifetime, and thank goodness we were brave enough to say yes and willing to work—*hard* to figure it out.

So many agents are offered opportunities, but they get complacent. They're not always willing to put in the hard work it takes to seize that opportunity. When I see an opportunity, I think: *What am I going to do with this?* And then I get creative and figure out how to make it happen.

Lesson #4: I will work with you, but I will not work for you.

In 2015, my dad was diagnosed with terminal cancer and passed away nine months later, leaving me a pretty big mess to clean up. My life coach, Kimberly Ryan, gave me a profound piece of advice that helped me cope with grief and the difficult emotions I felt around his death, including some resentment for the difficulties he left behind to handle.

"There are things your dad taught you to do, like how to be a good father and have a generous spirit. But there are also things he taught you *not* to do. You have to take both of those and run with them."

My dad did not teach me how to manage money. When he got sick, I realized that he had spent the five years that we were in a down market selling massive amounts of houses to investors, building their portfolios and their wealth. *I wish he would have applied some of that ingenuity to himself.* He always worked extremely hard for people, but for very little money, and he let his clients drag him around all over the place. He allowed himself to be abused for the sake of client services.

This was a turning point for me. I adopted a new mantra:

I will work with you, but I will not work *for* you.

We all need to make money and we can all become wealthy investing in Real Estate. I don't let anyone drag me around like a pet or speak down to me. Most real estate agents are so focused on trying to convince a client to work with them, that they will make all kinds of concessions in order to secure the sale.

I think this is mainly due to a lack of confidence. No matter how long you've been in this industry, you bring a valuable skill set to the table. Never forget that. By reading this book, you'll have a whole new set of skills to confidently guide your clients through even the most complex situations.

Lesson #5: The real estate community is financially illiterate.

Real estate agents are taught how to sell houses and make a commission. We are not taught how to maintain financial stability as we ride the real estate roller coaster—or how to pay off debt, save up reserves, or create a financial plan for our future. You need to create long-term financial goals so you can reverse engineer your current investment strategies to meet them. This requires you to understand how taxes work in different scenarios, how to choose properties to invest in, how to write off the depreciation, and how to leverage the liquidity and equity of the houses you own.

First and foremost, you need to understand that you should be your own best client. After all, you're out in the market, you understand the complexities, you're helping your clients take advantage of the best opportunities. Why wouldn't you also do that for yourself?

When my dad died, I chose to put the oxygen mask on myself for my family. I realized that I could still serve my clients at the highest level. I also learned to include myself when serving my clients, as I am a client as well.

This concept usually confuses agents. When working for an investor who's looking for a property and you come across a really good deal, do you automatically think, *which client should I bring this to?* Rather than, *Is this an opportunity for me and my long-term plan?* If you find yourself in a situation like this, the person who should have the first rights of refusal is *you*.

Remember, you don't have to choose between being a real estate strategist and being a traditional agent. Your traditional business provides you with a ton of opportunity to solve problems for people, which in return, brings you opportunities to buy properties for your own portfolio. As you'll see in many of the real-life scenarios I share with you throughout this book, once you understand how to go from agent to problem solver, you'll be able to create solutions that benefit your clients and yourself at the same time.

This all sounds great, and I bet a part of you is thinking, "I don't have the money to buy real estate, even if I wanted to." The most common fears that hold agents back from investing are actually based on myth. Once you understand how to structure your portfolio, your properties will begin to finance themselves. In the next chapter, I'll share some stories that illustrate this power and break down the barriers between you and the financial future you can't afford to miss out on.

As you read this book, I want you to remember these key points:

- Good agents are made in tough markets.
- Work *with* your clients, not *for* them.
- When you see an opportunity, say yes and figure it out later.
- Remember, if you want something, you have to work for it.
- Financial literacy is about understanding the true power of your real estate license and then using that knowledge to be your own best client by investing in real estate for your long-term wealth.

Chapter 2
Five Myths We Need to Bust

Just prior to the pandemic, I traveled across the country to speak at conferences and events, I met thousands of industry professionals. I discovered that on average, only about 5% of the real estate community actually owns or has invested in real estate beyond their primary residence. Yet 100% of them have sold or will sell an investment property to somebody, most likely many times in their careers.

This statistic is sobering. Most agents cannot properly guide their clients through the investment process because they've never themselves been an investor. Also, most agents will miss out on opportunities to grow their own wealth because of fears based on stories they've heard from other people about the pitfalls of owning multiple properties.

The sad reality is that most agents don't even consider investing in real estate because they believe in too many myths.

"I don't have the money for a down payment."
"I don't know how to manage it all."
"What if my tenants trash the properties?"

Sound familiar? I've experienced all of these, particularly in the early days, after we lost everything after the family business crashed. We all have the tools to build wealth.

Let's bust some myths!

Myth #1: I don't have any money to buy real estate.

Remember my story of how I got into REO accounts and changed my entire financial future? Remember, I didn't have any money either? I was heavily in debt, had lost my home to foreclosure, and was on the brink of bankruptcy. Remember I have always believed in saying yes and figuring it out later? Well, here we go.

The reality is that every person has five people in their sphere who have liquidity and are willing to lend it if you can present them with the right opportunity. To illustrate my point, here's a story about the first investment property I bought after the market crash. The experience changed my entire mindset about the myth of not having the money to buy.

A potential client, Jim, was a lead from Zillow. He inherited a house from his grandmother. Jim flew in from North Carolina to walk me through the house one Sunday morning. The house was a mess. It smelled like smoke and needed about $10,000-$15,000 worth of work to get it ready for sale. I valued it to list at about $160,000, repaired. As I walked through the house, like a typical real estate agent, I broke down what he needed to do to get the house ready for sale.

"You're going to need to get someone in to clean it up, and then you'll need to put in $15,000 or $20,000 thousand dollars to repair everything. By the time you're done with all of that and pay commissions on the sale, you'll be looking at about one $110,000-$115,000 net." I figured the house would sell within about ninety days on the market.

I remember thinking to myself, *what if I offer to buy the house for a lower price?* I'd already given him all the facts, the realtor terms, the timeline... everything. I knew the house was going to be a huge pain in the ass for Jim, because he lived out of state. Sooooooo..... He might be motivated to accept a lower offer for greater convenience?

Then again, it might just piss him off. I figured, what's the worst that can happen? He'll get mad and not list the house with me? I could live with that. By this time, we were walking out of the house. I was so nervous I couldn't even look at the guy, but I mustered up my 10 seconds of courage and said, "Hey, what if I gave you $100,000 for the house? You can just walk away." For a few seconds, he didn't say a word. I'm thinking, *Yep, he's definitely pissed off at me.*

He turned to me and said, "Give me $102,500 and it's yours." We still own that house. An amazing family has been renting it ever since!

This is where a lot of agents miss opportunities because they don't ask themselves, "What is the real problem that needs to be solved in this conversation?" Remember, not everybody simply wants to get the most money out of the sale. If the client had said, "Hey, you know what? I'd rather put the money into the house and then sell it for a higher profit because I could really use some extra money," I would have helped him down that road. But I recognized that his need was to unload the property quickly so he could fly back to North Carolina. Because I asked the right questions and showed him the options.

Here's the funny thing about this story: I actually didn't have the money to buy that house. I signed the contract with Jim on the hood of his car. I didn't have the money for a down payment, I didn't have money to repair the house—I didn't even have good credit! I didn't have a solution yet, so... say yes and figure it out later. If you find the opportunity, you'll find the money.

That following Tuesday, I was playing racquetball with my mentor, John. I told him about the house and asked him, with all the same nervousness I had with Jim, to loan me $110,000 at 10% interest to buy this house. He said yes, too!

Over the next twelve months, things got really interesting. I started to learn how I could use real estate to open one door after another. In this case, I gave up the $4,500 commission I could have earned selling that house and instead, bought myself $50,000 in instant equity. That equity grew and became the down payment for the house when I refinanced it. The strategy I teach is how to buy at a discount, add value, then refinance at 75% loan-to-value out of the private capital/hard money and into a mortgage. It's how we built an 86-home portfolio with very little of our own money. I'm getting ahead of myself, more on that later.

This was a huge epiphany for me. This is when I figured out that everything I perceived about not having enough money to invest was a myth. See, you don't have to save your own cash for a down payment in order to buy a rental, if you look to your sphere of influence for someone with cash who is willing to invest with you, then you just need to find the person most motivated to give you the best deal on a house you know you can rent, and refinance.

Myth #2: My tenants will damage my properties.

I currently own 86 single-family rental houses, right now. In the last ten years, we might have had one house severely damaged by a tenant. Is the risk always there? Sure. But think about the risks involved when you invest your money in the stock market. The way I see it, if damage happens, it's just a bad day in the stock market.

I was a tenant for five years in the property I rented after we lost ours to foreclosure. That house became our home. We have great memories there, and we took care of it as though we owned it. There is a stigma attached to renters, as though their status as someone who isn't able to buy a home somehow makes them less trustworthy. That is both unfair and untrue.

It all goes back to the golden rule of being a landlord, which is to ask yourself, "If I were my tenant, how would I want to be treated?" Do you want to be the kind of landlord who doesn't make repairs in a timely fashion, or are you going to take good care of your property? When you take care of people, they take care of you.

When you take care of your house, you will attract tenants who become as much of an asset as the property. Your tenants will be willing to pay a higher price to live there, and they'll stay longer.

When people tell me horror stories about bad tenants, I always ask them to take me back to the beginning of where they found the tenant in the first place. Did they hire a property manager to properly vet the tenant? No? Well, did you check references, etc.? Usually, bad experiences with tenants have everything to do with a lack of due diligence. Take my advice: Always hire a property manager. Their fees are a small fraction of the price you'll pay if you try to do everything yourself. (My staff calls property management fees "insurance premiums".) When your property manager finds a tenant, treat that tenant with care, and they will, in turn, take care of your house.

Use a property management company!

Do you know how many people don't own rentals or keep their homes as rentals because they think they have to manage the tenants, repairs, etc.? This is the most common comment I have from clients. I am a licensed agent and could very easily manage my portfolio myself. Instead, I have aligned myself with the right management company who takes care of my properties. My reasons:

1. Reduce liability: Every state has a landlord tenant act. This outlines the rules of engagement and what you are responsible for as a landlord. Do you know all of the rules of engagement? I don't. I do know

there are some pretty stiff penalties for not following them.
2. Protect your real estate license: Placing a management company, as an owner agent, gives me a layer of protection between me and a tenant.
3. Stick to what you are good at: You are probably great at what you do and you make great income doing it. Why would you mess with something you can pay 5%-10% of the monthly rent to cover you and your time.

    Example: You will pay $2000 annually for a company to manage and take on all the responsibilities of a $400,000 asset. That is .5% to manage the asset and not have to worry about it. This is a no brainer!
4. Peace of mind: While you are on vacation you don't have to worry. While you are at work you don't have to worry. When something goes wrong, you don't have to worry.
5. Save time and money: We get paid way more to do our daily job than I ever would dealing with any BS a tenant might throw my way.

What makes a great property management company? They believe the Tenant is as much of an asset as the property itself. Good communication skills with you, the tenant, and the vendors. Good relationships with tenants mean longer leases. The longer the tenant stays in a property the less turnover expenses you incur.

You want a full-time property manager. You want someone

who specializes in this industry and is not distracted by other income producing business ventures.

Example: You buy an investment property from your agent who also offers to manage it for you. What happens to your asset when he/she/it/them are showing houses and you have a water leak and the tenant can't get a hold of anyone?

Cheaper is not always better!

Another partner that we cannot do without in our rental portfolio is our insurance agent. When was the last time you received a call from your homeowner's insurance to review your current coverages? Your insurance agent is supposed to watch your back, but many insurance companies get you set up and you rarely hear from them again. You should have an annual review with your insurance agents across the board. Homeowners, auto, rental, and life policies. You are building your legacy through this process and it should be protected, unlike my client Mike who was referred to me after a $300,000 loss.

Mike was the money guy. He was approached by an acquaintance who found a great property to flip. Mike funded the deal and his partner was going to take care of renovation and managing the project. Mike was extremely busy with his own company. Guess what he and his partner did not do? They never put insurance on the property when it closed and the unfortunate thing happened. It burned to the ground and everyone left pointing fingers at each other. Needless to say, Mike and his partner are no longer partners. Mike suffered a $300,000 loss because he not only didn't have insurance but he didn't have a process in place when he purchased that house.

We are fortunate enough to have great insurance partners who watch our back along the way. Remember COVID when the price of materials shot through the roof? There were many homeowners and investors who suffered losses to storms, fires, etc. for which their properties were not insured for replacement cost. Having annual meetings with your insurance representatives is extremely important.

Myth #3: Debt is bad.

Inspiring Story: Tami, My Company's CFO

One of my goals with my own team is to help each of them buy real estate. I want to see them increase their net worth. With my CFO, Tami, and her husband, it took years to get them to comfortable with the strategies that we were using. They worked on getting debt-free. Now, how could they make their money work for them, too?

After 5 years of conversations trying to change their mindset around the fears holding them back, especially around cash flow, it happened. Close to the end of 2020, one of our agents came in with news of a property For Sale By Owner close to the office. I went over and talked to the homeowner, and I bought that house at a great discount. The minute Tami saw the address, she latched on to that house. She wanted it for her personal residence.

> She and her husband bought the home from me as their primary residence using VA benefits while keeping their original home—which was free and clear of a mortgage—as a rental. They then did a cash-out refinance (yep, more debt) and reinvested that money into another condo they recently closed on and rented. In the last two years, they have increased their net worth by half a million dollars. That debt they don't like? Tenants are paying that off for them.

In order to build wealth through real estate, you'll need to borrow money. We have been convinced a mortgage is a necessary evil for homeownership, and we should pay it off as fast as we can. Yet your home's equity opens the door to investment opportunities. To access that equity, you'll need to borrow against your home. The only other way to do it is to sell your house, and that defeats the purpose of what we're trying to do. If you understand how to discern what makes a good investment property, and you know how to structure your finances, you'll be able to control your cash flow around your debt so you can leverage your properties to grow your portfolio even further.

Soon, you will guide your clients to do the same. A lot of homeowners will say things like, "I've heard that home equity loans are bad. What about all the interest I'm paying? Now my mortgage will go back up, and I want to pay off my house." Some homeowners may have already paid off their mortgage and may be reluctant to go back into debt. They see this as a big step backward, and it paralyzes them. Your job is to show them the financial benefits of using debt strategically when buying more income-generating properties.

FIVE MYTHS WE NEED TO BUST

There are ways to feel more secure and confident about investing. I will show you examples of how to make your properties' cash flow so that they largely pay for themselves. It's also vital that you build financial reserves so you always have a safety net (we'll talk more about how to do that in Chapter 4).

When people talk about real estate, they say things like, "I put 20% down, but I have no cash flow!" Maybe they're even in the negative $100 a month. If this is your current fear, let consider this: Your Individual Retirement Account (IRA) and your traditional investments are most likely invested in the stock market and mutual funds. Neither one of those common investments give you cash flow yet, you're likely more willing to put, say, $500 a month into them. Are you willing to put $500 or even $200 a month into a physical, long-term asset that's always outperformed every other type of investment?

I totally believe that investments should have cash flow. I think they have cash flow at a certain time in life. Right now, you have an income. You don't necessarily need cash-flowing assets until they become your main source of income. That's why we start with your long-term goals, and then reverse engineer your investment strategy to meet those goals.

Think about the answers you wrote down in the "Wouldn't It Be Cool If" exercise. What do you want in five years? In ten? What monthly income do you want when you retire? In Chapter 5, you'll learn how to use your answers to create your own investment strategy.

Myth #4: I need to time the market just right.

Everybody wants to try to time the market. THERE IS NO SUCH THING! If you look at the law of averages, you see why this is true.

Let's use my first house as an example. I paid $107,000 for it in 1999. Five years later (2004), it would have cost me $200,000 to buy the same house. Just three years later (2007), prices had dropped so far that the same house was now worth less than what I paid for it originally. At the end of those eight years, the value of that house averaged out to somewhere in the middle. When you understand this, you'll realize how fruitless it is to try to time the market. Currently, in 2023, that house is worth over $425,000.

One of my biggest Aha! moments was when I realized that I was short-sighted. Again, this goes back to financial literacy. Instead of worrying about what the market is doing, focus on things you can control, like your spending habits. So many agents increase their spending habits as their commissions go up instead of putting money in reserve for future opportunities that can arise at any time.

Most importantly, cultivate good *saving* habits so you always have a financial cushion. Set up regular contributions straight from your bank account to a savings account that you never touch, and you'll be surprised how quickly funds accumulate. Like I always tell my coaching clients, a dripping faucet will fill a bucket over time.

When you're not distracted by chasing that next commission to pay your bills, you can stay laser focused on your search for properties that meet the criteria of a good investment. This will free you from the unpredictable ups and downs of the market and shift your attention toward things that have a far bigger impact on your current and future wealth. Instead of worrying about what the market is doing, turn your attention to creative problem solving so you're ready for the next big opportunity.

My dad once told me, "From the time you got your license in 1999 to where you are now, you've seen more market changes and shifts than I ever saw in my entire lifetime." Just by reading this book, you're learning all those cumulative lessons, which I hope will change your entire financial future.

Myth #5: Investing is too complicated!

A lot of confusion and fears around owning multiple properties can be addressed by structuring your portfolio correctly and knowing all the things that you need to be prepared for. You need to learn two things.

1. What to buy.
2. How to manage & protect what you bought.

After buying, selling, and renovating so many houses throughout my career, I can walk into a house and instantly assess whether it's worth my time. Even with something like a hoarder situation or a repossession, which can easily scare off a new investor, I can usually tell whether the house is a tear down, or whether most of the damage is just cosmetic. I also have a good sense of how much it would potentially cost to renovate the house to rent or resell.

The more you practice and look at deals, the greater your skill set and confidence develops. You'll recognize a good opportunity. You will become more comfortable with risks and quicker at backing away from something when the numbers don't work out. Part of my Limitless Real Estate Strategy Tools, which I go through in Chapter 5, includes what I call the Buy Box.

Every investor has their own Buy Box, which is essentially the definition of a perfect house to add to your rental portfolio. Your Buy Box is a set of criteria that you will start to define as you read this book, list properties, and represent buyers. Once you determine your Buy Box for flips and/or rentals, you can search for properties that fit that description. Knowing what to buy is already taken care of. Investing has already become less complicated.

For instance, my Buy Box includes mainly single-family houses close to home. I like shingle roofs and I don't like pools. I prefer single story houses and I'm not a fan of multiple HVAC units. In our area, 3 bedrooms rent better than 2 or 4. I look for older houses that may need repair—hoarder houses or repossessions are usually a great fit for me because Wende and I have extensive experience fixing up tired houses.

When developing your Buy Box, your criteria may be completely different. It needs to be based on your experience and comfort level with risk. It also needs to evolve as your portfolio grows, on what the market is like, where you want to invest, and what type of houses typically rent best.

If you're not already familiar with the rental market in your area, ask a local property manager. They know exactly which properties make the best rentals and can help you dial in on things like how much rent you can expect, how long tenants typically stay in each house, etc.

Which brings me to the second thing you need to learn. How to manage all the properties you own without getting overwhelmed?

You don't have to manage everything yourself. That's what a property manager is for. Once you reach the point where you can't, or don't want to, handle the logistics of your rental properties, you can turn the management over to a professional. Who finds and vets tenants, collects deposits and rents, manages repairs, and most importantly, correctly and legally manages the rare worst-case scenarios. You'll need an accountant, too, and a lawyer that understands the complexities of real estate investing. For now, let's stick to property management.

Remember, you have everything you need to debunk real estate investing myths right here in this book. Together, we're going to start constructing your big picture plan.

Chapter 3
From Agent to Problem Solver

Everyone has to find their own path in this business. My path may not be the same as what you ultimately settle on. The key that unlocks the door to limitless possibility is when you shift from the mindset of a traditional agent to the mindset of a *problem solver*.

Every client you speak to has a unique situation, with unique variables that affect their decisions. It's our job to unlock the conversation with the right questions, in order to truly solve their problem. For one client, the best solution might be for them to put their house on the market and sell it traditionally. You might be able to buy their house from them, or you may advise them to keep the home and convert it to a rental. But if you're not giving your clients options—if you're not truly solving their problems—then you're a salesperson.

This also means you will be a traditional agent for your entire career with no additional options to offer.

My definition of a salesperson is somebody that's trying to convince someone else to buy something they may or may not want. As agents, we run the risk of falling into the darker side of that definition whenever we fixate only on the commission. I've always believed that being an agent isn't about selling. As an agent, I can't really sell you a house. I can show it to you and guide you through the process of buying it. Ultimately, the house sells itself. Consumers buy houses based on the way the house feels, the way it looks and smells, and whether they can see themselves living there. My job is to guide and problem solve so each client makes the right choice for their unique situation. This is where agents forget what their true value is.

There's always more than one way to accomplish what any given client wants to accomplish. The problem is, most clients don't actually *know* what they want to accomplish. That's your opportunity: you can give them clarity on what they want, show them what's possible, and guide them as they make the right decision for themselves. Give them options!

When you learn to be a better guide, you can help more people. You can see beyond the limitations they think are insurmountable. If inflation hits too hard and your client suddenly decides they can't afford a house because the interest rates are too high—which is happening as I write this book—you can say, "Okay, so maybe you can't buy a $750,000 house right now, but you *can* invest in a house that is less expensive. By the way, let's look for something you can live in now and keep as a rental later on. Let's not give up dream home ownership. Let's just change the path to that dream home. When you consider purchasing a home, you become an investor, and from that point forward, both you and your clients are investors in the real estate space.

Ask the right questions.

When I meet a new client, the most important thing to determine is: *What is the real problem that needs to be solved?* The answer is not always to simply get the most money possible out of the house. Remember the house I bought from Jim? The most important thing to him was selling the house as quickly and painlessly as possible. He was looking for the easiest way out. I gave it to him and he was grateful. Agents are often too fixated on trying to sell themselves to the client. It ends up being a "me presentation" rather than what I call a "strategy session."

I ask questions like:

- What do you need?
- How much money do you want to make out of this?
- Have you considered options other than selling?

When I mentor my coaching clients, I bring them into my client conversations and let them look over my shoulder as I problem solve my way through different situations. With each situation, there are so many unique twists and turns. Each consumer has different questions. Often, when an agent comes to me for help with a situation, they're not sure how to handle, I get on the phone with them and their clients and problem solve our way through to a strategy together. This allows my coaching clients to actually experience the conversation, learn how to answer questions, and find creative solutions to different scenarios.

FROM AGENT TO PROBLEM SOLVER

Develop situational awareness.

Learning through observation—just like I watched my dad negotiate deals back when I was a new agent—helps my coaching clients learn perhaps the most important skill in this business, which I call situational awareness.

Situational awareness is all about understanding conversations and knowing how to put things in perspective for your clients. When agents seek out my coaching, it's typically because they need help negotiating with sellers to get the best deal, especially in challenging or unusual scenarios. They're looking for solutions that benefit everyone in any given situation. Let me show you an example of how I helped one of my coaching clients, Jack, change his mindset from agent to problem solver by letting him join me live on a Zoom call with his client.

Jack's client was a trustee who lived and managed two houses in Arizona from out of state. Jack met with the trustee and discovered the houses were trashed; these were some of the nastiest houses he'd ever seen. Jack wasn't 100% confident about how to have a conversation with the seller about the options he knew were available.

I suggested we get the trustee on a Zoom call and walk through all the options. Jack wasn't in the position yet to be able to buy the houses himself—each house needed at least $150,000 to $200,000 in renovations. This was still an opportunity for him to create income from the sale to an investor... me, as Jack knew I was interested in buying the houses, for the right price. During the Zoom call, we presented all of the same scenarios I did with Jim. When it was time, I made an offer. I asked the trustee, "If I buy both of these houses for $700,000, does that ease the pain of trying to repair the houses, rent them, and manage them from afar?"

The trustee accepted my offer, and I negotiated the deal right on the call. Everybody wins! The win for the trustee was a no-hassle sale. The win for Jack was $50,000 in commissions. Had he just listed houses on the market, he would have made maybe $20,000 in commissions total because the houses were in such poor condition.

The win for me? I had planned to renovate and flip both houses. After crunching the numbers further, Wende and I weren't willing to take the risk with the project load she had at the time. I re-sold the houses to one of our partners who also does flips. Because I was in the position of being able to purchase those homes on the spot, we ended up netting about $250,000 profit on those houses over the following fourteen days.

After working with me, Jack is now prepared to capture the next opportunity like this when it comes his way. I do buy a lot of deals from my coaching clients as they bring them in. But eventually, I want them to be able to go out and seize opportunities for themselves. It all comes back to being prepared.

The opportunities will look different, depending on what stage of your career you're in. Stage one as a new agent is all about doing traditional commission sales and earning income. Stage two is where you're not ready to invest, but you can still find creative ways to earn more income, just as my coaching client did. He earned $50,000 in commissions in seven days by bringing his clients' properties to an investor—me, in this case. In stage three, you have the knowledge, the money, and the mindset to be the investor yourself. You start getting paid to connect the dots for your clients and build your legacy.

Recently, I interviewed two of my longtime friends, Kevin Kauffman and Fred Weaver, co-founders of Group 46:10 Network and the professional membership community, Next Level Agents. For the past fourteen years, Kevin, Fred, and I have met for lunch monthly to swap stories and share industry advice. I asked them, "If you could go back, what would you have done differently?"

Before I could even finish my question, Kevin blurted, "Buy more real estate!" After all those years having lunch together and listening to me tell stories about the properties I was buying, Fred and Kevin wish they'd followed my lead sooner.

"We were so focused on making sure our system was what it was and the team what it was. But if I could change anything, it would just be to take an extra minute or two a week and look at the deals coming through my inbox and buy one or two of them a year."

I was also fifteen years late to the game, so I'm making up for lost time as fast as I can. If you're like me—or Kevin or Fred—and are learning these strategies later in your career, my advice is simple: Get started today. You can never fully make up for lost time, but it's also never too late to start.

Chapter 4
The Problem-Solver's Mindset

You don't know what you don't know. And you don't know what you haven't been taught. My goal for this chapter is to help you shift your mindset from *I can't* to *How I can?*

Your relationship to the industry is critical to your success. To fully understand how to make this shift, you need to understand how the traditional real estate mindset differs from the approach I'm teaching you.

Like my dad, my coaching clients come to me with the typical industry mindset, which is limited to doing business focused on only *one* thing: commission sales. When an agent gets their license, they think, "I want to make six figures a year showing pretty houses!" They're constantly looking for the next commission rather than the next opportunity.

Most agents are driven by these two goal mindsets their entire career:

1. Transaction count (i.e., the sale)
2. Gross Commission Income or, GCI

What if, instead, you ask yourself these questions:

1. What are my income goals?
2. How many families do I want to serve?
3. How much wealth do I want to create?
4. How much net worth do I want to create?
5. How much net worth do I want to help my clients create in the investment space?

As agents, we've got to get over the buy/sell transaction and start asking ourselves how we can help more people and how we can better help ourselves. And then we need to turn around and teach more people these same strategies. It starts with changing your mindset about what it means to hold a real estate license.

The mindset shift I invite you to make will allow you to serve more clients, help them make better informed decisions and allow yourself to create generational wealth. It all starts with changing your mindset about what it means to hold a real estate license.

Mindset Shift #1: Step away from the leaderboard.

Traditional agents are customarily only taught one way of doing things. They don't understand the true power they hold in their license.

Agents tend to be driven by leaderboards and competition. They're so distracted by making the next sale that they don't truly consider how best to actually *help* their clients. Selling a bunch of houses doesn't mean you'll actually have anything to show for it at the end of the day, especially if you never take advantage of the opportunities that cross your desk.

When someone asks me what I do for a living, I say, "I'm a real estate strategist." A real estate strategist, or problem solver, constantly looks for creative new ways to accomplish the buyer's or seller's goal. Strategists ask questions and listen to get to the heart of every situation, and then present all the possible solutions to the client. We don't sell; we guide.

The goal is to figure out the seller's net number—how much cash they want to walk away with at the end of the day—versus simply giving the seller a list of all the added costs of selling the house (i.e., commissions, closing costs, etc.). If you figure out the seller's net number right out of the gate, then you can pinpoint how much room there is for potential repairs, renovations, upgrades, etc.

For example, it costs about $50 per square foot to renovate a house, which means a seller needs about $100,000 to put a 2,000-square-foot house back together. Most sellers don't have those funds and will want to know what they can get out of the house without touching it. If you know the seller's net number, you can present them with their best options. One of those options might be to sell the house to you for their net number and walk away.

The real estate industry tends to be ego driven. A bunch of accolades won't pay your bills or build long-term wealth so you can retire with something to show for your career.

Fred and Kevin see numerous opportunities come into their brokerage everyday with the network of agents they have cultivated across several states. When you are ready and looking for the opportunity, they will appear from some of the most unlikely of places! These days, Fred and Kevin each buy a new property every twelve months or so, to add to their families' legacies.

In Phoenix, other agents come to me to help them fix all sorts of crazy scenarios. Why? Because I'm known as a problem solver. I'm teaching my "competition" to do what I do, and my goal is to help them build wealth and improve the industry as a whole. Those relationships also provide opportunities for me, and we all gain valuable learning experiences.

Mindset Shift #2: Be prepared for the opportunity. Are you ready?

One of my favorite quotes is by Warren Buffett. He said to be "fearful when others are greedy, and greedy when others are fearful."[1]

To me that translates into my best advice: Be prepared for opportunity in *any* market, because there *is* opportunity in every market. Luck is when opportunity meets preparedness. Wende and I own a piece of land where we plan to build our dream home in the mountains. We bought the land a few years ago for about fifty cents on the dollar, it has quadrupled in value since then. We were able to buy this property because we'd spent years doing the mindset work

---

[1] Warren E. Buffett, "Chairman's Letter," address to Berkshire Hathaway Inc., February 27, 1987, https://www.berkshirehathaway.com/letters/1986.html.

to have the creative strategies—and, yes, the money—at our disposal.

Which brings me to the first, and maybe most important, piece of advice I can give you: Be disciplined enough to *not* spend every penny you earn, and *save* at least 10% of your income. Don't live expensively. Remember the real estate roller coaster? Never fall into the habit of spending more as you earn more. This is how you get ready!

Whether you invest your savings or just tuck it away for now in a bank account that you don't touch, get in the habit of putting away a little bit of money all the time. Get in the habit of saving early on, and you can change your entire financial future. Remember my favorite adage: A dripping faucet will fill a bucket over time.

> Tip: I highly recommend looking into Whole Life Insurance with a banking policy. We discovered these a few years ago, and it is a great place to keep tax savings and reserves, plus has numerous other benefits.

I always say that if you won't save ten dollars out of one hundred, you won't save $100 out of $1,000, you certainly won't save $100,000 on a million- dollar income. So, start with that first $10 and make those good habits early in your career so one day you can do what Wende and I did and buy a dream property to build your retirement home on.

Last year at Thanksgiving, I asked my mom: "Did you and Dad ever have a financial reserve or savings account?"

THE PROBLEM-SOLVER'S MINDSET

Her answer shocked me. "Never in our entire life."

Of course, this all changed after my dad's passing, and my mom and I have worked hard to make sure this is never an issue again. But sadly, this is all too common. Never let yourself get in a situation where you're desperate for a sale just to pay the bills. The goal I recommend is to save three to six months in reserves. It takes time and discipline to build that up, but a reserve fund will make sure the bills are always paid and buy you time to pivot your business if you need to.

Right now, we're going through a shifting market. A lot of people have lived fat and happy the last few years, and they haven't put reserves away. The more money they make, the more lavishly they spend. Vacations, cars, clothes, new furniture— their spending habits go up right along with their income.

I coach my team members and my coaching clients to never put themselves into a situation where they're forced to make knee-jerk reactions when the economy fluctuates or money gets tight.

Over the last seven years while the market was really good, we took a majority of our income and dumped it back into assets. So now, we have reserves, and we have liquidity. Yes, it takes some discipline to do that; you have to be willing to accept delayed gratification. I want you to understand that this is a marathon, not a sprint.

In the real estate industry, everyone wants to live off transactional goals. How many houses do you want to sell this year? How much money do you want to make? Agents will say, "I want to sell one hundred houses and make a million dollars." Then they'll spend half a million to make that million. There's never a net worth goal.

I set goals based on the income I want to make. What I want you to see is that you can generate income in multiple ways beyond just commission from a sale. I have a goal for how much I want to increase my net worth every year. Nobody puts you on a leaderboard for how much money you've got in the bank, or what your net worth is. Just because you sold a bunch of houses, doesn't mean you have anything to show for it. My dad was a prime example of that.

If you have debts, face them head-on. I know as well as anyone how painful it is to get up close and personal with a bad financial situation. In order to solve money problems, you need to have a clear picture of where you stand, no matter how ugly that picture is. Don't bury your head in the sand.

When I faced foreclosure, I relied on three things to avoid bankruptcy. First, just stubborn pride. We had personal notes for $100,000 to several people who were counting on us to pay them back. For me, my character depended on staying true to my word.

Second, I was proactive with my creditors. I sat down and made a three-page spreadsheet of every debt I owed, with account numbers and contact information for each creditor. Every couple of weeks, usually as a payment was due, I called to update them and always let them know ahead of time if I was going to be late making a payment.

When most people get into debt, they start ignoring the problem. They stop paying bills, and let things go to collections. One of my biggest debts was a second mortgage for $140,000. In the end, I hired an attorney to settle it for me, which took several years to finally close. In the meantime, I paid $24 a month for two years just to keep the bank off my back enough to keep the account open and prevent it from going to collections.

Lenders are people, just like you. I always found that the more I communicated with creditors, the more willing they were to work with me because I was making an effort. They got nicer. At the end of the day, people honor effort. Often, a simple phone call is all it takes to negotiate some breathing room. Even if you can't make a payment, it's far better to give your lender a heads-up instead of just skipping the payment. Be clear that paying down the debt is a priority, and ask if they can work with you while you figure out how to improve your situation. It took me four years to pay off all my debt; it was a daunting task, but I got there and so can you.

The third thing that helped me avoid bankruptcy was my work ethic. Whenever my dad would talk to someone who worked forty hours a week and was still broke, he'd say, "And what are you doing with the other forty hours that you could be working?"

He was right. If you're in a tough situation, how hard are you willing to work? How will you pay off your debts in as short a time as possible? I come from a family of workaholics, so this comes naturally to me. Anyone can do it. Sometimes in life we have to work hard. That's just reality.

You want that pair of Air Jordans? Go out and work for them.

Mindset Shift #3: Be cautiously optimistic.

As agents, we're the first ones to see the market slow. We're so entrenched in the complexities of the market, but the general public needs to be educated on what's actually happening. They only see the talking heads and the news and the fear.

Agents fall into this trap, too. In a tough market like we have right now, agents will all of a sudden get "commission breath." Their sole focus is on selling so they can get paid and be able to pay their bills. Their clients are equally fear based, and everybody gets Chicken Little syndrome.

"The sky is falling!"

Now everybody is doing exactly what people do in the stock market, which is, the minute the market starts to drop, they instantly pull out thinking it's going to get worse, rather than being patient and letting things sit.

If you don't have to sell a house in this market, my advice to you is to keep it as a rental or stay put. Unless you're relocating or something similar, there's no point in selling right now. Be patient. There is no perfect timing in the market ever. Last year, some people said, "I'm going to wait until the market cools down before I buy." Well, the market

THE PROBLEM-SOLVER'S MINDSET

did cool down. But what nobody planned on was for interest rates to double. Now, those people can't afford to buy. It was actually smarter for them to buy *last* year at a higher debt with a lower interest rate because they could afford the payment. We all buy things based on payments, not on the overall debt.

This is why your clients need you to be the voice of reason—to help them see past the negative hype and bring them back to making the best decisions based on their needs. *You* need to keep your head in the game so you can spot opportunities that inevitably arise in a market like this...hell in any market!

Remember when I said that good agents are made in hard markets? If I can buy houses at eighty cents on the dollar in the most outrageous market we've ever seen, then I can certainly get great deals as the market starts to shift. But I have to have the right mentality.

That's the mentality I didn't have in 2008 because I was so focused on generating income so I could afford everyday living expenses and not drown under my debt load. If I could go back knowing what I know now, I'd do things differently.

I go back to that Warren Buffet quote: "Be fearful when others are greedy, and greedy when others are fearful."[2]

---

[2] Warren E. Buffett, "Chairman's Letter," address to Berkshire Hathaway Inc., February 27, 1987, https://www.berkshirehathaway.com/letters/1986.html.

Well, people are scared right now, which means that this is where you find your gold mine of opportunity. Consumers need your cool-headed wisdom right now when so many other agents are selling doom and gloom, and that's going to cause some consumers to make very bad choices. Your clients need your cautious optimism. It's tough because real estate is a game of opinion, which makes optimism hard sometimes. This is why mindset is so important.

Stop sitting on the sidelines waiting for the perfect or ideal timing of the market. While the lowest interest rate for a mortgage in history came in 2020-2021, the lowest annual mortgage rate on record was in 2016, when the typical mortgage was priced at 3.65%. They were so low I don't know if we will ever see those rates again in our lifetime. If you purchased a home during this time for $500,000 at 3% interest, the principal & interest payment on a 30-year note would have been $2,108. That market was fast and furious. Buyers were paying above list price and sometimes over appraisal and giving up all your rights as a buyer. No one expected what came in 2022! Interest rates doubled and the prices stabilized or, in some places, fell slightly. If we use the same $500,000 house, the price may have dropped 10% and market value is now $450,000. The price dropped, but the interest went up from 3% to 6.5% which makes the payment $2,844.

This is over $700 a month more in payment on a house that costs $50,000 less! Sure, the price is lower, who cares if you are in this for the long haul! Someone else is going to give you the money for the payment, the tenant when they pay their rent. The lower interest rate and higher price serves your long-term goals. In fact, it is better. Waiting for the lower price means the house no longer has positive cash flow on the rental market.

Let's go back to perfect timing if your goal is to own 10 properties and you buy 1 a year or 1 every 2 years you will pay less for some houses and more for others. Thats the way the law of average works. Some payments will be higher and some lower. They eventually average out. Example: Remember Jim the Zillow lead. I paid $110,000 for his house in 2015. In 2022, 7 years later in the same subdivision and similar square footage I paid $300,000 for a similar house. Both houses I bought below current market value but my average is $205,000 for the houses when looking at the big picture. My average mortgage payment between the 2 houses is $1,200. One has a higher cash flow than the other, but that compensates enough of the second's negative cash flow to make them both great investments.

When I paid $110,000 for the first house, I said, "Do you know I could have purchased this home in 2009 for $50,000?" Then in 2022, I could have purchased this home for $110,000. There is no perfect timing only working the end goal of how many properties and how does it fit into your long-term strategy.

Mindset Shift #4: Put your ego aside and hire good people.

The best way to maintain a winning mindset is to get support from a mentor or coach—someone who has walked this road before you. If you don't already have a mentor or coach, well, this book is a great place to start.

My podcast, *The Real Estate Revolution*, is another resource that's packed with advice from the top experts in the industry, as well as client and agent interviews. If you want more personalized guidance, you can work with a coach, either one-on-one or in a group setting, to help you succeed. You can also get in touch with my team to book a discovery call so we can figure out where you go next. Whatever you do, get support and save yourself the pain and trouble of trying to figure everything out on your own.

I've always worked with a coach, which is probably the number one driving force behind my success. Even when I was in financial ruin, I worked with a coach. Remember the story of how I pivoted my business into foreclosure accounts after the market crashed? It was my business coach who gave me the confidence I needed to seize the day and run with it. I also bought my first investment property because my longtime mentor loaned me the cash. If it wasn't for my coaches and mentors over the years, I'd probably still be chasing the leaderboards and living commission to commission.

Let me tell you a story that puts this all-in perspective. My dad always told this story whenever he wanted to teach me about the importance of not quitting. Back when he was busy diversifying into all the construction companies, he used to meet with a business consultant once a week. In 2006, the consultant told us to shut it all down. "Just get rid of those companies, and focus on real estate," he advised. "You're losing so much money." My dad refused. He said that would be like quitting two feet from gold.

THE PROBLEM-SOLVER'S MINDSET

His gold story goes something like this:

A family moved to California during the gold rush, betting everything on the promise of striking it rich like the stories they'd heard. They started to dig and found nothing. No matter how hard they worked, all they turned up was ordinary rock and disappointment. There was no more gold.

Desperate to recoup some of their losses, the family sold the property and all their mining equipment for pennies on the dollar. Shortly after, the new owner struck gold.

A year after my dad passed, I came across the *actual* story in a book, and was shocked to read the *real* ending—the crucial part my dad always left out:

After the new owner bought the gold mine, he hired a geologist to go down into the mine and track the vein, to figure out exactly where to dig. He followed the advice of the geologist, and soon after, struck gold.

See, the new owner didn't strike gold by coincidence; he found his riches because he hired an expert to steer him in the right direction. The moral of the story is, you need to hire somebody smarter than you to guide you to where you want to be and where you want to go. The point of my dad's favorite story has nothing to do with the family giving up too soon—just two feet away from gold. The point is that they failed because they were digging blind. They would have struck gold, too, if they'd hired somebody with greater wisdom than they had.

Hire for your weaknesses. My CPA, for example, saves me more money in taxes each year than it costs me to hire her.

Her knowledge of real estate taxes has also enabled me to find new strategies for buying and selling, including the timing of each purchase and how to maximize tax incentives only available to people with a real estate license.

Similarly, a lot of people don't see the cost of coaching as an investment. Yet, that investment can save you years of trial and error and put you in front of opportunities you might never have found on your own. Somebody asked me on Instagram the other day, "If I had $10,000, where should I invest it in real estate?"

Invest in a coaching or a Blueprint strategy session with me!

You have to be willing to invest in the knowledge you can get from experts in your field. I probably spend six figures a year on coaching and mentoring, to make sure that I stay aligned with my goals, mindset, and where I want to be in my business. Some people are not willing to look at that as an investment, or they hire the wrong coach and that expense becomes a loss.

Good people are an investment, not an expense.

One thing that I love about what I do is that I'm still truly active as an agent. So, I have the ability to guide and coach in real time, rather than based on theory gained from what I learned from another market or another period in time. Everything I coach is based on the realities of today.

Remember, good agents are made in tough markets. Without a mentor or coach to guide the way, a hard market just might break you. Invest in yourself so you can thrive no matter how hard things get.

Chapter 5
The Limitless Strategy Tool Box

Now that you understand the difference between a traditional agent and problem solver, and you've made the mindset shift to that of an investor, you're ready to build your roadmap. In this chapter, I'll teach you the tools I use to help both agents and client's structure and execute their wealth-building blueprint.

Once you learn these tools, not only will you be able to build your own portfolio, you will also understand how to guide other people to invest in properties, which will increase your traditional income. Remember, this isn't about selling; your job is to present your clients with potential opportunities, explain the benefits of investing in each specific opportunity, and then help guide them through the purchase.

When I guide someone through the process of buying an investment property, I can do it with confidence because I've experienced that process myself while building my portfolio over the years. Most investors come to agents with a preconceived notion of what they want to buy. The investor ends up guiding the agent, instead of the other way around, and the result isn't always the best outcome the investor could have had.

The more properties you buy, the greater the expertise you bring to the table for your clients, and the better your conversations. Eventually, you'll become known for your expertise, clients—and other agents—will seek you out to learn from you. Your relationship capital will grow too. The inevitable result is increased business and volume of sales.

> ### *Inspiring Story: David and Taylor*
>
> I now get to introduce you to David and Taylor. Three years ago, we were visiting with good friends David and Taylor. They asked me if I'd help them buy their first home. At the time, they were expecting their first child. Two days later, they found a house—he used his VA loan to buy the home for $250,000 with no money down. The goal, I explained, was not to nest there long-term. The purchase was step one of an eighteen- year strategy designed to create a college fund for their child.
>
> Twelve months later, I came back and said, "Okay, it's time to move." They refinanced about $100,000 of equity from the first home, using that to buy their second home. Twelve months later, their second home also gained $100,000 in equity. Today, they own two homes and their net worth has increased by $350,000 in the last three years.

Let's fast-forward fifteen years into the future. Let's say the numbers are exactly the same, and David and Taylor still have $100,000 in equity in each house. Rather than selling a house to pay for college, or contribute to a 529 college savings plan (please investigate the 529 savings plan) they can do a cash out refinance on the first home to use some of that equity to cover their child's education, all while the tenant continues to cover the payments of those debts.

There are three advantages to this plan:

1. Rental income will still cover the debt on the first house.
2. There is no capital gains tax consequence for selling the house.
3. Leveraging the house creates a college fund in which *they* control the destiny. The return on investment is exponentially higher than that of an educational savings plan.

By the way, their houses will continue to appreciate as long as they own them. The debt continues to be reduced as the tenants pay rent to cover mortgages and expenses.

Real estate offers a high return of investment while being affordable compared to other investment opportunities. This is why it's so important for you to develop an investor's mindset right from the moment you purchase your first home. The first home you buy is not the home you're going to live in forever. It's a house that you rent from yourself to create long-term wealth and generational change. This is how you build a legacy!

When you stop focusing solely on your commission and learn the power of real estate, suddenly the possibilities are limitless. Once you understand the complexities, you can explain them to your clients to help them develop an investor's mindset, too.

As you help clients build generational wealth, you'll also build long-term relationships with buyers who come back to you again and again to help them build their portfolio. That's how you turn a one-time client into a lifetime client.

So, let's take a look at our Tool Box!

Reverse Engineer the Goal

The first step in investing is to answer two questions:

1. How much passive income do you need monthly/annually to fulfill your dream life without having to work another day?
2. At what age do you want to achieve that goal?

Decide how many cash-flowing assets you'll need and by what age, and whether you want to own those assets free and clear or leveraged. The more passive income you want to achieve, the higher the ratio of leveraged properties to free and clear properties will be.

Next, we figure out how many properties it will take to get you to that goal by your target age. Calculate how much rental income you'll be able to collect from each property, other costs associated with each property (i.e., renovations, repairs, upkeep), how much money you'll need for the down payments, and the debt required to buy them all.

Now break that down into a plan with quarterly, semi-quarterly, or annual goals to work toward. I always recommend people buy at least one property every 12 - 24 months, your strategy will depend on your cash flow—which can fluctuate—and your age. If you're in your twenties and you decide you need to buy a dozen properties, you can accomplish that with a bunch of thirty-year mortgages and be done with it. On the other hand, if you're like me and got a late start in investing, you'll need to buy more frequently in order to reach the same number of properties.

Let's look at an example to illustrate this process.

Paul and Susie are thirty-five-year-olds, and their goal is to earn $10,000 a month in passive income by the time they retire at age sixty-five. They will need to own ten houses, free and clear, that each produce $1,500 to $2,000 a month in rent in order to create that income. Now, if Paul and Susie leverage, they will need to own twenty houses, each mortgaged at a 50% loan-to-value in order to produce the same amount of income.

If Paul and Susie start right now and buy one house a year for the next fifteen years, they will be able to produce that $10,000 a month in residual income. Since the average life of a mortgage is thirty years, they will own some of their properties free and clear, and some may still have a mortgage attached. The values of each house may also fluctuate over the years, but Paul and Susie will stay the course, buying one house per year no matter what the market is doing.

When you reverse engineer your own plan, remember that part of your cash flow comes back as a tax benefit because of depreciation of the houses. You need to consider the difference between cash in the bank, and what your property saves you each year in taxes, and how that accumulates over time. This is why it's so important to invest in a CPA (certified public accountant) that understands real estate and the tax strategies that real estate investors can use.

Build the Structure

One of my coaching clients is young and newly married. We sat down to help him structure his portfolio correctly right from the start so he's not backtracking down the road. Your marital status affects the way you should structure your purchases, so it's important to understand the limitations and advantages of your different options.

First off, if you have a spouse, do you both have incomes? If you both have incomes, you should buy one property in your name and the next in your spouse's name. Federally insured loans (Fannie and Freddie) have a limit of 10 per individual. If you buy properties combined, you can only finance 10 traditionally. If you put them in individual names, you now have access to 20 loans. Your goals for the number of houses you want to acquire will dictate this.

If you're single, you may have to collect assets more gradually. In either case, make sure you hire a lawyer to help you set up a trust so you have a plan for your assets and they are protected. The more properties you own, the more important it is to do some careful estate planning, especially if you have children.

You also need to structure your business correctly so it generates income. Many agents will flip a house and get excited about all the money they made. Yet their business structure doesn't actually create the income they think it does. It comes back to financial literacy, which means seeing beyond the income claims you see on HGTV where they'll show someone making, say, $100,000 on a flip. They never break down the numbers and mention the costs you need to deduct, like the cost of sale, taxes, etc. If you're in a 30% tax bracket, you'll have to pay $30,000 in taxes on the sale right off the top.

Rather than flipping houses for profit, what if you instead add value—enough value to create your next down payment? You don't have the tax liability, you don't have the cost of sale, and you're creating generational wealth for your future so you're not still doing open houses at age sixty-five.

This is how we structure that. You are one of three or four people in a transaction when you buy a house. I think of myself as different business entities or personalities in each transaction.

There is Steve, the **investor**. $

Steve, the **buyer's agent**, found this property for Steve, the investor. I need to pay Steve and his company to represent me on the purchase of the property. $$

If I flip or do repairs on the house, I have to pay contractors. Wende is the **general contractor** for our renovations and most repairs, I pay her company for that service. $$$

I also pay Steve, the **selling agent,** his commission when the house sells. $$$$

I generate income in 4 different ways. For my real estate company and construction company while also building my personal wealth. As an investor, my goal is to make $10,000-$50,000 per property. So, after all expenses are paid, my company is paid to be the real estate agent for the transaction, the construction costs are paid for the flip, I operate just like any other investor does where costs are concerned. This includes the off-market deals

It's important to realize that if you're getting a big check from a house flip but not making your company financeable/bankable, you create a disadvantage for yourself down the road by not structuring your entire enterprise correctly up front. If you have employees, you need a way to pay them, this is where the profits from your investments come into play. You need to understand the complexities of taxes, and the implication of every transaction on all the different facets of your business as a whole, as well as how everything works together to build your personal wealth. Again, a crucial part of the process is having a good accountant and lawyer on your team.

The Buy Box

I teach the Buy Box as a set of criteria to help agents discern what makes a property a good investment. Your Buy Box is unique to what type of properties rent well where you live (or where you invest) and what your short- and long-term goals are. Do you want to buy a townhouse or a single-family home? Do you want to try the vacation rental market or traditional rentals? Maybe you're thinking about buying a whole apartment building. The Buy Box is a method of assessing every opportunity so you can decide which properties are right for you.

Something to consider is the location of your properties. I invest close to home so I don't have to travel to my properties. I know the market and it's easier to manage renovations on fixer-uppers, repairs, and tenant relations.

As a new investor, you might be thinking, "I don't want to buy houses that are in poor repair. That's so much extra work!" Fair enough. Wende and I had that fear in the beginning, too. We are fortunate enough that Wende took on the general contractor role because we can take advantage of a lot of deals on houses other investors might shy away from.

Before Wende became a licensed contractor, she managed the process in the same manner you would. She started by building a team of dependable contractors, including plumbers, painters, electricians, etc. This was the path to our success. Just like building a real estate team, you have to build a contracting team you can trust.

If you're not able to start out this way, then maybe simplify your investing approach so your Buy Box only includes houses that are ready to rent. That can change over time as you gain experience and confidence. The key is to decide what works best for you now, and then get started.

In the early days, we would buy houses, fix them up, and sell them to other investors as rentals. Eventually, we started keeping some of them. The more we learned about construction, the more expertise we could offer our clients, too.

Here in Phoenix, Arizona, I know exactly what to look for. I prefer single-family homes, and I prefer older rather than newer. In fact, hoarder houses are my favorite investments. Wende manages the renovations of our fixer-uppers, and we work with a team of reliable tradespeople that we've built great relationships with over the years. We know how much money to invest in each house, how much rental income we can expect, and roughly how much we could sell the houses for if we decide to flip or pull equity.

I try to stay away from houses with pools because they're a long-term liability. It's cheaper to demolish a pool than to maintain it over the years. I don't usually buy condos either, but they might be a good investment where you live, so long as you steer clear of condos with high Homeowners Association (HOA) fees. We rent our properties as homes rather than vacation rentals, although we've done both.

My favorite properties are anything with the potential to cash flow, especially if it's a particularly good deal. If I buy something at a discount and it needs work, not only do I have to have the down payment, but I also have to have the cash to renovate it.

If you're unfamiliar with the rental market you want to invest in, reach out to local property management companies. They can educate you about the going rental rates for each type of property and how much to expect in operating costs. By the way, you don't have to invest where you live. I only buy properties that are local because everything is easier for me to manage close to home. You can invest anywhere you like, as long as it makes sense for you financially and you have systems in place to properly manage your assets.

To determine your Buy Box, answer these questions:

1. What is the rental market like in your area?
2. Do condos rent better than houses or the other way around?
3. If you're considering a condo or other STR (Short Term Rental) property, what are the HOA fees?
4. Are your properties located in an area where there's high demand for vacation rentals?
5. If you decide on short-term rentals, do you have someone to manage the property so you're not involved in the day-to-day operation?
6. Does the house need renovations? If so, how much will it cost?
7. Would this property work best as a long-term investment or a short-term one?
8. How much operating capital do you need for the type of property you want to invest in?

Here is an example of our Buy Box and the reasons we have chosen them. Our buy box was created to reduce long term liability and maximize the efficiency of major repairs.

- **Close to home:** This makes them easy to manage and drive by if there is a concern. We do not invest in other states or markets we are not familiar with.
- **Single Family Homes:** Condos and Multi-family usually come with an HOA. This makes the

property more expensive to qualify for and maintain. Some Multifamily (Condo's) properties have restrictions on rentals.

- **NO HOA:** this makes properties easier to manage and rent. Strict HOA rules equal violations and extra tenant management and cost. The money that goes into an HOA is a lost investment. That money can go toward a larger purchase, supplementing a non cash flowing property, or paying the loan down quicker.

- **No Swimming Pool:** The only person who benefits from a pool on a rental is the person who is paid to clean it every week! They are a liability that make insurance rates higher and when an insurance company will cover them. The cost is less to demolish a pool than it is to maintain. There is also the concern of more equipment to replace when it breaks and replastering when the time comes. Over a 30-year period a pool can cost you up to $110,000 to maintain!

- **Single Air Conditioning Unit:** 3-4 Bedrooms or around 2000 Sq. Ft. is the size of the house we like to keep. It's a numbers thing, If I have 2 units, I want to be collecting rent on 2 Houses! More than 1 unit means replacing more than 1 unit as well. Bigger houses bring less rent per Sq. Ft. for rental (just like sale).

- **Composition Shingle Roof:** Shingle roofs are less expensive to replace and maintain.

Put the Plan in Place

You can't hit a target you can't see. Once I learned what made an ideal property for me—location, length of time for tenant, etc.—my target was identifiable every time I went to an appointment. So, whenever a seller asks me to help them sell their house, I look at the house and consider whether or not the house is a target.

Putting your plan in place is really about being able to label your targets and being prepared for opportunities that fit your definition of an ideal property to add to your portfolio. With every house that fits your Buy Box, there are multiple options. Is this something you can flip? Is it something you can turn into a rental? Or is it something you're just going to put on the traditional market? If you don't know your targets, you won't be prepared to make your presentation to the seller about the different options available to them either.

The Buy Box identifies your targets in terms of what you want to own for the rest of your life as generational wealth. Your Buy Box will change as you move forward in life and get closer to your end goals. In my case, we've always focused on small, single-family homes, turning them into rentals or flips, and we've learned so much from that portfolio. It truly is the easiest place to start.

As we grow, our target changes. Recently, I looked at a thirty-three-unit hotel that can be turned into short-term rental units. We are potentially going to scrape a $2 million house and build a destination VRBO. Everything goes back to using your tools. Over time, you have to revisit your strategy and pivot as your target starts to change. The approach might change, but the goal will always be the same. To create passive income and create generational wealth through Real Estate holdings.

> ### *Inspiring Story: My Coaching Students, Kacia and Seena*
>
> I met Kacia through a mastermind group. At the time, her husband, Seena, was working on his exit from dentistry, a profession he was no longer satisfied with. He wanted to get into real estate. Six months later, we sat down over dinner, and they shared the news that Seena's father had just passed, leaving him with seven or eight pieces of property. Some were vacant lots, one was a house, and another was a townhome. All of them were a surprise so he didn't' have the luxury of coming up with a plan beforehand.
>
> I was so honored to be brought into the conversation. People who know me know that it's never about a sale— it's the strategy and the advice that I can give them that they value. All the property was out of state. At the time, they didn't know anything about investing and had no idea what to do with the legacy Seena's father had left him.
>
> We spent the next couple of months strategizing about how to move the pieces around. In the meantime, Seena and Kacia relocated to Denver, and Seena was working on obtaining his real estate license. I showed Seena all the options available. Did he want to own the properties free and clear or did he want a seller carry-back? Did he want to look at creative financing or sell things outright? They coached with me for six months, mapping out their plan until the pieces fell into place. They were able to do creative

financing on the house, which was still mortgaged when Seena's father died, and they sold one of the lots, which gave them money to move into other cash-flowing assets.

They bought their first rental in Phoenix, again using creative financing. They found the Buy Box house, I bought the house for them, and they bought it from me. We got such a great deal on the house that after a couple of months, they refinanced it and ended up with about $150,000 in equity in their first rental property.

I recently got a text message from them to say that they just bought a million-dollar four-plex in Colorado. Seena found a seller who would do a seller carry-back at 4% and they put $100,000 down. Using the strategies I've shown them, Kacia and Seena are using real estate investing to create income and legacy.

Make a Lasting Impact in Real Time

"That's what I consider true generosity: You give your all and yet you always feel as if it costs you nothing."
—Simone de Beauvoir

There is one question I've asked hundreds of real estate professionals:

Did you know that your real estate license gives you the knowledge and power to create your own legacy of wealth?

The answer is always this:

"Show me how to do that, Steve!"

So, I have a question for you.

Would you do something that takes one minute if you knew it would help someone else create a legacy of wealth for themselves and their entire family? Or if you could change someone's life? Build lasting professional relationships? Change their relationship with money? Be a better leader? Create a ripple effect that's bigger than you? If so, I have a favor to ask you.

There are people all over the world who dream of building a business that creates a lasting legacy—not just for themselves, but for their clients, their colleagues, and their families. The knowledge I share with you in this book can help people in a way that creates a profound ripple effect. But the only way to create that ripple effect is to reach people. So here is what I ask:

If you've found this book valuable so far, would you please take sixty seconds right now to leave an honest review wherever you bought the book? This costs sixty seconds of your time and could be the reason someone chooses to start investing in themselves by investing in real estate.

All you have to do is say yes, and you are participating in a movement that will help your family and the families of others for generations to come.

More people believe their dream is possible, and the more people who learn the tools and strategies I teach in this book, the better the world will be.

Together, we are changing the world one person at a time.

If you decide to leave a review right now, thank you. You are part of the movement. As you read the rest of the book, you'll learn even more strategies to help you weather the ups and downs of the market and harness the power of your real estate license so you can achieve incredible success with your business, your wealth, and your life!

Just remember, a ripple effect can't always be seen, but it can always be felt.

Thank you for your help. I appreciate you!

Chapter 6
People Over Profit

I've built my business off the strength of my relationships, not off the client relationship manager (CRM), although I regret not working my CRM better than I have. You might have been trained that the CRM is the end all and be all, but in reality, the CRM is a system and task manager that will help you have better communications and track your progress. The one thing the CRM won't do is help you with your conversations, and conversations are the key to relationships and your success. I have good conversations with people and put their needs as humans before everything else. I'm a problem solver, and I get paid to do it. Over time, people have come to rely on me to help them with life situations that go far beyond simply buying and selling houses.

When you own properties, you have the ability to provide homes for people within your sphere. You can help people in a crisis, who might otherwise find themselves without a place to live. Maybe they're experiencing divorce or have lost their rental home because their landlord sold the house. As you'll see in the stories I'm about to share, over the course of your lifetime, your impact on other people's lives can be profound.

Someday I will write a book with nothing but real estate stories (I have thousands) and share with you some of the craziness I've seen and clients I've met. For now, here are a few I want to share with you now.

> ### The Twins' Story
>
> Back in about 2015, my son, Christian—who was twelve years old at the time—came home from school with concerns about some classmates.
>
> "Mom, Dad, we have a set of twins in our class. And they've been wearing the same clothes for a while. I'm not sure what's going on, but it seems like their family doesn't have any money. Is there anything we can do?"
>
> A week later, I found out that the twins' parents were getting a divorce. The home they lived in was owned by the husband's family and the family had kicked the wife out with her four kids. Without an affordable home to move into, she and her kids were struggling. We happened to have a house that we'd just finished remodeling to keep as a rental. The house was essentially brand new and a perfect fit for the mom and her four kids. We were able to reach out to the mom and say, "I think we can take care of you here." She was so grateful! She moved in shortly after as a paying tenant and has lived in that home for the last seven years.

The coolest thing in the world was when Christian got a text just months ago from one of the twins, who is now a young adult. The message said: "Hey, because of your family, it changed everything for us going forward."

Through owning properties, we were able to change the trajectory of that family and have a profound positive impact on their lives. Because of our portfolio of 86 homes, we're able to help people on a regular basis. The payoff is huge, both on a human level, and financially, because the more problems you can solve, the more houses you're going to sell.

When you own real estate, you have the ability to fix things for people.

The Crocus Story

Here's another story that illustrates how you can have a positive impact on someone's life when you leverage the power of your portfolio to help people. I call it The Crocus Story, named after the street the house was on.

When I buy a property, I don't always have an exact idea whether I'm going to rent it or flip the property—I just buy first and figure that out later. But in this case, I bought the Crocus Street house to flip. The house was a referral from a friend of mine, whose family had inherited it from their elderly mother. It needed a lot of work on the exterior, including a new roof and major work on the pool, plus other things the family wasn't prepared to fix or pour money into. The inside of the house, though, had been very well kept, despite being out of date.

We had just started to get bids on this house when I got a call from a coffee shop owner near our second home, "Hey,

> can you help this person out? A woman who runs an animal rescue here just lost her house in a fire. She has four big dogs and nobody wants to take her lease because of them. She's desperate to find a home!"
>
> Insurance was going to pay three times market rent for temporary housing for her and her dogs. Despite the financial incentive, nobody wanted to take the lease. I looked through my inventory of houses and thought of the house on Crocus. Instead of flipping that house, I called the coffee shop owner back and said, "I happen to have a house that we just bought and might work. It's perfectly livable, and I don't care if the dogs do any damage, because we're going to renovate it anyway."

The house on Crocus became the perfect solution for a woman whose life was otherwise in disarray. I was able to put her into the house quickly, and she stayed there for a year until she'd settled with her insurance company and was able to find a permanent new home. In the meantime, the value of that house increased by 25% in the year that we rented it, and the rent covered all of our costs during that time.

You see how cool this is? Because I put people first and I am known as a "dot connector," people call me to solve all kinds of problems for others right in my community. I could have easily said I didn't have anything suitable, and I don't want four dogs in my house. But I put the person over profit, I was actually more profitable in that scenario. The end result is that we'll probably make six figures on that house.

When you become a problem solver, everybody benefits, including you.

> ### The Flagstaff Story
>
> You never know when a new mutually beneficial opportunity to help people will come your way, which is why it's so important to be prepared financially and with the right mindset.
>
> In the middle of the pandemic, I bought a house from a landlord who had lost his job and was desperate to sell. I was able to buy the house with the tenants in place. Afterward, I went over to meet with the tenants just to see what their plan was. I'd bought the house to flip, but again, putting people first, I didn't want to evict them without knowing something about their situation.
>
> "Actually, we've been thinking about buying a house and relocating to Flagstaff," they told me. That weekend, I took them to see some properties in that area and sold them an $800,000 new build. Toward the end of their lease, after they'd already given notice and were in the middle of relocating, they found out that the builder was six or eight weeks behind schedule. The timing couldn't have been worse—they were trying to get their kids settled in new schools in Flagstaff.
>
> I had a furnished VRBO in the area, so it to them for three months. They stored their belongings in the garage in Phoenix—I had a new tenant move in, and just worked with both families to get everyone settled, including the kids,

until the new house was finished. It worked out for everyone involved, and because I took the time to meet the tenants in the beginning rather than just evicting them to flip the house, I also gained new clients and sold them a house.

When you put people first, you can increase your income and gain repeat clients.

The Uber Driver Story

People are humans, which means you need to find ways to work with them so everyone benefits, especially when times are hard. During the pandemic, we had one property where the tenants couldn't pay the rent. They were trying, but they were Uber drivers and basically lost their income during the lockdowns.

We went for seven months with no rent, but we kept working with them and helped them complete the paperwork to apply for government assistance. Eventually, that assistance kicked in and paid eighteen months in full, covering the back rent and several months in advance. We were patient and things worked out for all of us.

People over profits means you need to be flexible. The payoff is that everyone benefits, including you.

To me, putting people over profits really comes down to guiding rather than selling. I always refer to that first meeting with a new client as a Strategy Session rather than a traditional listing appointment. Although it means giving up on a potential commission from a sale, my first guidance is always for a client to keep the home as a rental property if they can. I'll help them decide whether that is a viable option, and whether it makes sense for their future goals.

Most people are short sighted—they want to know how much they can get by selling their house. Instead, you can coach them into keeping the house and buying something else then, repeat that process in another year or two. If you can teach somebody how to move from one place to the next for their first ten years of marriage—if you can show them the advantages of putting off that short-term gratification for the sake of a better long-term plan—you can actually increase your sales significantly. And you'll help your clients build a plan for generational wealth in a way that probably never occurred to them before.

Sometimes it's not possible for a client to keep their home as a rental and buy something else to live in. If you were in their shoes, wouldn't you rather be able to explore those options? Show your clients the options on paper. Help them determine whether they have the reserves to hold both properties. Explain the process and help them see how the cash flow works and help them adjust their mindset around being a landlord. As an agent, always ask yourself, "How do I lead and guide my clients to their best life?"

Throughout your career, I want you to get emails from people who say things like, "I'm so grateful that you helped us figure this all out." "Because of you, we just sent Jimmy to college without incurring debt!" When you educate your clients about how to create an investment portfolio that's good for their future, when you show them what's possible, you can change the trajectory of their lives. The ripple effect can span generations.

What a great position to be in! I love what I do. Every day, I get to show people what's possible and then help them set their plans in motion. This is the power you hold with your real estate license once you understand how to use it. Remember, you don't have to give up traditional real estate in order to expand your business into other avenues, like investing, flipping, wholesale, etc. You can incorporate them all into your day-to- day business.

One last very important point I'd like to make about putting people over profit: *Don't forget to put yourself first, too.* A big part of that is being true to who you are. That can be as simple as showing up to work every day in clothes that you're comfortable in. I'm a jeans-and-t-shirt guy all the time. It's the way I show up on social media, it's how I show up at the grocery store, and it's how I show up at my clients' front doors.

When you are true to yourself, you are more confident and comfortable in all of your conversations and interactions. Whether it be in person, on social media, or on a Zoom call. Other peoples' opinions of you are not your concern.

Just show up as you are, and you'll attract people into your sphere who resonate with you. It's the easiest—and best—way to build a personal brand.

Chapter 7
Let Your Clients Choose Their Own Adventure

The first time I meet a new client, I never go to the appointment prepared. Yes, you read that right. I never show up with a folder or a briefcase prepared to convince the person to list their house with me. I'm not there to share how many houses I've sold or how quickly I can sell them. My objective is to put on my guidance hat and ask questions to get a baseline of what the person is looking for, and then give them strategies. I do look at the neighborhood first and have a general idea of how much the house is worth, but until I've seen exactly what condition it's in, I can't fully gauge the market value.

I go into each appointment to build a rapport. I'm a problem solver. Remember, most potential clients are looking for somebody to guide them and aren't even aware of the different options that exist.

My job—and yours—is to present the best options for each client based on their situation. I offer guidance and then let the client choose their own adventure.

LET YOUR CLIENTS CHOOSE THEIR OWN ADVENTURE

Let's talk about Jim (Chapter 2) again and walk through this process together. The story is a good example to use for this purpose: it represents a lot of the houses you'll come across day to day, and the most common options you'll offer your clients. If you remember, the house belonged to a potential client from out of state who found me through Zillow and flew in to sell the house he'd inherited from his grandmother. I didn't have a prior relationship with the seller, but I wound up buying the house on the spot at a deep discount with cash borrowed from my mentor. This house was my first investment property after the market crash—a "say yes, figure it out later" opportunity—and it taught me to leave my agent hat at the office and go into each appointment as a problem solver.

The first step is always to ask the right questions—go through all the what-ifs. In this case, the grandmother had passed and left a house in disarray. After I assessed the approximate renovations costs at between $15,000 and $20,000, I asked:

- Do you have the funding to make the repairs to the property?
- Are you prepared to manage contractors from afar while you renovate?
- What's your ideal timeframe for the house to sell? Is it sixty days? Ninety days?
    - Have you thought about fixing it up and keeping it as a rental?

- What if I had an investor who could pay in cash as is, no closing costs, no commission - what would your net number be?
- Do you understand the tax consequences of selling this house?
- Has it been owner occupied for more than two years?
- What does the equity look like in this house?

Based on his answers, I narrowed his best options down to three scenarios:

1. Fix up the house and sell on the open market
2. Sell as is on the market
3. Sell it to me

Scenario #1: Fix Up and Sell

If the homeowner had chosen this option, I would have connected him with a property management partner. I always advise people to hire a property manager so they don't have to be involved in the day-to-day duties as a landlord. But in this case, the house was in Arizona while the seller lived in North Carolina. Managing the property himself wasn't feasible.

Next, go through the pros and cons of keeping the house versus selling from an appreciation standpoint: tax implications, possible strategies, and future passive income.

LET YOUR CLIENTS CHOOSE THEIR OWN ADVENTURE

Questions to ask:

- What's your current mortgage payment?
- How long have you owned the property?
- Do you have reserves? (Note: For my first five houses, I kept a reserve fund of $5,000 per property.)
- What is market rent in the area?
- What repairs need to be done?

Sometimes after asking these questions, the client may choose not to go with this option, in which case you can help them proceed with one of the remaining two options.

Scenario #2: Sell As Is

Based on your client's situation, they may choose to sell the house either as is or repaired. In my client's case, he would have had to spend a significant amount of money to repair the house to get the best price on the market. Some clients won't have the funds to renovate to sell, which is a great opportunity for you to buy the property at a discount.

A word of warning though: As real estate agents, we often buy ourselves a job and put ourselves in harm's way when we offer to get directly involved in fixing up a property to sell.

Here's what I mean. Say your client chooses to fix up the house and sell it. Your goal is now to sell the house, not to become a general contractor. In order to get the listing, a lot of agents will take on jobs they don't get paid for. They'll offer to connect the client with contractors, and then step in and manage the renovations. If the renovations go wrong and you've paid the contractors up front, you can wind up on the hook for the renovation costs and possibly in legal hot water with the client.

In Jim's case, it might have been very tempting for me to say, "You go back to North Carolina. I'd be happy to manage everything for you here. I'll pay for the repairs and reimburse myself out of the proceeds of the sale." By offering to act as general contractor, I would have secured the listing and hopefully listed at a higher price—maybe even made extra profit.

I've also experienced the opposite. I once referred a seller to a tile tradesman that I'd used in the past. The seller paid a deposit, and the tile tradesman took the money and never showed up. Maybe you help your seller coordinate a house painter, but when the job is done, the seller hates the paint color and refuses to pay the invoice. The seller never hired the painter—you did, and now you're responsible for the bill.

When this type of thing happens to us as agents, we feel the need to compensate the seller because we made the referral. So, I've just chosen to take myself out of that realm. I want to help people, and it's especially tempting to take on the job as a contractor when your client is out of state. There's so much liability in it. I do not advise it.

This is exactly how we ended up in so much financial trouble in 2007. My dad saw his clients as a captured audience and a chance to build the business with other vertical layers. This is when we ventured into the trades and construction. To him, it made perfect sense. The reality was, those companies bled the company's profits. When the market crashed and real estate sales could no longer cover the losses of my dad's side businesses, we were ruined. If you feel confident giving your clients a list of suggested contractors to call for estimates, go ahead, but urge you to not get directly involved, especially when it comes to paying for the repairs.

I learned a lot from that time in my life. The big realization down the road was; we didn't have the right people to manage those businesses. Today Wende owns the construction company, which is a great vertical for our investment. It's great for flipping and great for our clients. We have the right person to run and maintain that business, which is a profitable business, and adds value to what we do in the industry. I am no longer involved in the renovations or design, and it's great to be able to refer clients to her and walk away.

Scenario #3: Sell It to Me

Make an offer. The worst thing your client could say is yes, and then, you have to figure it out. I offered $102,500 to close the deal in 10 days and he could walk away without making repairs or negotiating BINSRs (Buyer Inspection Notice and Seller Response) repairs.

The Result: Scenario #3

This is the scenario my client chose after we went through all the questions above. Had he put the house on the market for $160,000, minus the cost of the sale and repairs, his net would have been $120,000 after about ninety days (30-45 days of that in Escrow). He chose to accept my offer of $102,500, close the deal in ten days, and walk away. He was open to a lower net because it meant he didn't have to put time and money into the other two solutions. He didn't have to come back to Arizona to wrap things up. He was done and done.

If I had come across this deal early in my career when I was stuck in the mindset of a traditional agent, I would have chased the buyer in order to double my commission. Instead, I chose to chase the money by providing an investor—in this case, my mentor—with a way to invest without the liability of owning the property, all while receiving a double-digit return on his money.

People tell me they're afraid to go around asking people for money. I get that. At first, I was afraid to ask my mentor of 10 years to loan me $110,000. I realized I wasn't asking for money—I was actually providing him with an opportunity to make money.

People who know you, love you, and trust you are more likely to take a risk on you when you present them with opportunities to invest. If you find a great property but don't think you have the money, get creative. Can you tap into your home's equity with a line of credit? Or look to your sphere of influence for potential investors: friends, family, mentors, former clients.

LET YOUR CLIENTS CHOOSE THEIR OWN ADVENTURE

Develop situational awareness. Ask the right questions and have better conversations. Understand each consumer's situation. When you step away from the mindset that there's only one way to earn an income as an agent, you open yourself up to a world of possibilities.

Chapter 8
Be Prepared to Pivot

Evolution in your career is a great thing. Change is inevitable—in the market, the global economy, even your personal circumstances. We're all afraid of losing our livelihoods, and some agents are so afraid that they don't embrace change at all. The better you set yourself up to be nimble, the more prepared you will be to pivot when the need arises.

Over the last 23 years, my business has completely changed iterations five times. My most recent shift into being a coach, speaker, and trainer has led me into the influencer world. At first, I was afraid that as I shifted my social media presence toward speaking to agents from the point of view of a coach, I would lose my real estate clientele. Truthfully, I probably did lose some clients. I also gained a lot of clients and a lot of knowledge from being willing to take that risk. If you know the direction you really want to take, you may lose a little bit by following that path. As you evolve and grow, you will gain far more.

Whenever people are scared to make a shift, they start asking, "What if?" My response is, "What if you do the scary thing and it turns out ten times better than you thought it ever could?" You could avoid making sacrifices of change and stay on the same path your entire real estate career, just as my dad did. If you really want to explore a new direction, don't let fear hold you back.

If you adopt the right mindset and structure your business to be nimble, market fluctuations can be a zone of opportunity for you. As I write this book, we're having a correction in the real estate market for the first time in many years. Agents who've only been around a decade or less have only known a good market with low interest rates. At the first sign of a change in the market, they succumb to the doomsday hype. They don't recognize the wealth of opportunity this new market brings.

That's what I missed in 2008. Although I missed out on all the real estate deals to be had, I did say yes to the opportunity to get into the real estate–owned (REO) market, which allowed me to rescue my business and my personal financial situation. I wouldn't be making six-figure profits on houses right now if I hadn't been willing to take that first risk and embrace change.

By about 2014, we started to see the foreclosure business slow down. In your business, whenever you see things start to shift, that's when you should turn your attention toward what's next. I started to consider the investment side of things and think about whether I wanted to go in that direction or just go back to traditional real estate. I realized that maybe I could do both. That's when the Zillow client came along, and I made my next big pivot into owning rental properties.

If you understand the investment side of real estate, you're able to pivot in down markets, when down markets happen, a lot of potential investor clients come looking for deals. If you teach people how to invest rather than being scared of things, there's so much potential to massively increase your commissions. Right now, I tell investors now is a great time to get in the market. "Let's buy some rental properties—rents are up, the rates are high, and it's cheaper for people to rent than it is to buy, which means opportunity for you." High rates also mean there are more motivated sellers in the market, and more choice, which translates into a higher chance of finding deeper discounts. You just have to hunt for them.

We may never see another situation like in 2008, unless there's a massive war or something of that nature that wipes out the economy, in which case everybody's in trouble. But it won't be a repeat lending crisis. Right now, we still have a supply and demand issue. The only thing that's changed recently is affordability.

My mindset is to stay open to the massive opportunity happening right now. If you know where to look for it and how to recognize it, you'll find ways to build your career and personal wealth *because* the market has shifted. This blip will pass, just like it did after the worst of the pandemic, and just like it did after the disastrous consequences of the market crash of 2008.

It's important to realize what really happened in 2008 and understand that what we're experiencing right now is nothing like what happened fourteen years ago. That market crash happened because of terrible lending practices—probably 90% of houses were 100% financed, (some 110%!) which meant that all the risk was on the banks. homeowners who didn't have any skin in the game just walked away from their mortgages. After all, it was much easier to fix their credit later. The banks were in a crisis because they suddenly had all these foreclosed homes on their hands but couldn't sell them.

Right now, I have ten houses on the market that we renovated. If I have $100,000 in equity in each of those, I'm not going to walk away from them. I'm going to try to sell them and get as much money out of them as I can. That's the difference in the current market: people have equity in their homes. This market wasn't built on fictitious loans. People have to put money down to buy a house, and their equity is driven by the economy and the market. It's a whole different ball game in comparison to what happened in 2008.

When you're thinking about buying real estate as an investment, it's also important to realize that appreciation of property usually outperforms index appreciation on the stock market, on average, with a way smaller cash investment up front. Even if your property value decreases as the market fluctuates, you've still got the asset. I would rather see my property go into the negative, knowing that my tenant is still covering the mortgage, than to see my stock portfolio plummet.

In the last three months, I've seen people lose 20% of their retirement savings, and all they can do is try to stomach the loss and wait it out. No matter what the market is doing, I know my houses are still being paid off, I'm building equity every month, and I can leverage them if I need to.

Here's a great example of what it might have looked like for investors during one of the toughest real estate markets today's agents have ever seen. Let's say you bought a house in 2007—which was the peak of the real estate market—and paid $200,000 for it. Say your mortgage payment was $900 a month and you collected $1,000 a month in rent. In 2008, the house decreased by 50% in value. Despite that, you wouldn't have had to change anything, except keep it rented. You might have had to lower the rent for a while. If you'd been able to ride it out, by 2017, that house would have been one-third, or 33% paid off, and its value increased by more than $150,000 from your original purchase price.

Learning to pivot also means keeping your cool when the market dips and everyone else gives in to negativity and fear. When change is outside your control, stay open to opportunity and be prepared to steer your business in a new direction. While others make fear-based knee-jerk reactions to shifts in the market, you can open new doors for yourself from a place of creativity, strategy, and confidence.

You also have to evolve with the market. So how are you pivoting with the market? Are you prepared for the opportunity? Are you seeing an opportunity? Or are you just running around like Chicken Little, saying, "The market is terrible! Nobody wants to buy or sell." Remember, good agents are made in tough markets.

The pandemic changed a lot of the world in terms of the way

BE PREPARED TO PIVOT

people view the relationship between home and the workplace. People have realized, "I don't have to go to an office, I can work from home. I can work in another part of the country and have cheaper living costs." What we haven't seen yet is the full impact of telecommuting. For example, a friend of mine is an executive with Discover Card. Before the pandemic, they had about 100,000 square feet of office space. Now they're down to 20,000 square feet because they've moved their workforce home.

Commercial space is not needed in the same way anymore. In my company, we've started to look at what opportunities might come from vacant commercial real estate. Again, it's a market pivot, and we constantly have our eye on how to evolve alongside it.

One of my favorite quotes is by Keith Cunningham, author of *The Road Less Stupid*. He says, "It's not what you see, it's what you don't see."[3] Right now, people are not seeing that this is a market of opportunity. Instead, they see it as a market of *fear*.

Wende's favorite quote is, "Perception is reality." Whether you see the glass as half empty or half full is all your perception. Right now, what I perceive is that there's opportunity, which means we're going to get busier, and I need more capital. So, I started having more conversations. Meanwhile, most agents perceive a shortfall. They wonder, "Should I start knocking on doors? Doing more open houses?" These are two very different mindsets, and both produce vastly different outcomes.

---

[3] Keith Cunningham, The Road Less Stupid (Keys to the Vault, 2017).

So, my question for you is this: Which perception is *your* reality? Look at what the market is doing, and how your business is evolving. Be prepared to pivot into new opportunities as the world shifts around you.

Chapter 9
Invest In Yourself

In Chapter 4, we explored what it means to have a problem-solver's mindset, which includes the willingness to invest in the knowledge you can get from experts in your field. I shared the story of the family who lost out on striking it rich in their California gold mine—not because they simply gave up too soon, but because they didn't hire an expert who could show them exactly where to dig. In this chapter, let's look at the best ways to invest in yourself, both personally and professionally.

First, let's get the purpose of these investments straight: it's to keep yourself accountable to your goals, and to give you those outside-the-box ideas that can help you take your business to the next level. Coaches, mentors, and masterminds are some of your best options for personal and professional guidance and growth, and you may decide to work with just one of those options, or all three.

I have coaches for different areas of my life. I have a trainer, for example, who helps me structure healthy eating and my workouts. My trainer holds me accountable for that one aspect of my life, which is why I pay more to help me in that area than just buying a gym membership. I also pay for accountability with different areas of my business.

It's important to realize that just like any property you buy, what you put into your investment is also what you will get out of it. You have to do the work. Your coach or mentor is not there to coddle your ass, and paying for their time doesn't mean you get to *waste* their time. Think about it in terms of this equation:

$$\text{Activity} + \text{Behavior} = \text{Productivity}$$

Coaches, mentors, and masterminds are all there to help you with different parts of this equation depending on where you need the most support. Let's take a look at the difference between them so you can decide the best fit for you.

Coaches

A coach is there to help you make changes in your business practices to get more out of yourself. The coach will help you identify your goals and then set metrics to keep you motivated and on track. In the real estate industry, you'll often come across coaching service offers at the end of conferences and training events to help you implement all the valuable information you just learned. I found my first coaching experience this way, with Tom Ferry. It was very activity driven and based on sales goals, which was great from an accountability perspective.

I think this is a great spot for an agent to start, because an activity-driven coach is there to help you make left or right turns so you can stay on track. If you're not hitting your sales goals, for example, do you need to make more calls? Set more appointments? Eliminate distractions? A coach will ask you the hard questions so you can get back on track to what you want to achieve.

Also think about whether you want to work with someone one-on-one or in a group setting. Group coaching is less expensive, and you may be timid about speaking up and about the questions you ask. You may also find that pressure from the group makes you more accountable. I caution you to make sure that the group you're mixing with is right for you. Even if the coach seems like a great fit, the wrong group can sabotage your efforts.

Mentors

A good mentor will help you grow into the professional you want to be. Mentorship is usually more behavioral focused than a coach. A mentor can help you change your mindset and build professional and personal confidence so you can achieve the results you want. They are there to share their knowledge with you on what made them successful.

To find a mentor, first decide what you need help with, and then reach out to people you admire who have had success in the areas you want to improve on. You can reach out and ask someone to mentor you, but you have to be very cognizant of their time. The head pastor in my church is mentored by John Maxwell, a well-known leadership author, speaker, and pastor whose personal time is in high demand. They meet once a quarter; my pastor sends the five things he wants to discuss ahead of time so he is succinct and respectful of Maxwell's valuable time.

Whether you pay your mentor or not, be respectful of that person's time. Never show up late, and come prepared with your questions and ready to implement what you learn. Remember, a mentor wants to help people. Be clear on what your needs are so they can help you as efficiently as possible.

Masterminds

A mastermind could be described as a business support group, where like-minded professionals get together and share their experiences, successes, and failures on a regular basis. Masterminds can be invaluable in putting things into perspective, and help you keep yourself accountable and looking forward.

I discovered the world of masterminds by accident when I picked up a book by personal development speaker and business coach Lewis Howes called *The School of Greatness*. I loved his story about how he built a multimillion-dollar online business after an injury ended his career in professional football. To figure out how to rebuild his life, Howes sought mentors and went back to the lessons from his former athletic coaches and applied everything he learned to his new business.

At the time, I didn't know anything about the influencer space, but I was so impressed with Howes, I told Wende, "I'm going to Columbus, Ohio, for a thing this guy puts together for entrepreneurs in all types of businesses." She was a little skeptical that anything of value to my business could be found in Columbus, Ohio, but I went by myself not knowing anyone and not knowing exactly what to expect from the event.

Talk about getting out of my comfort zone! My goal was to try to meet someone at every lunch, dinner, and happy hour. During the event, I met amazing people, who became good friends and introduced me to my current mentor, Chris Harder. I was also introduced to so many influential people across multiple industries. Through those connections a new world of possibilities has opened up to myself and my family.

Soon after, I was accepted into an Elite Entrepreneur Mastermind. I have participated every year since, furthering my connections and broadening my personal and professional goals.

When you invest in yourself, you invest in others, too. When I look for a mastermind, I search for groups that include people from all walks of life who can potentially influence, impact, or encourage me. I do not restrict myself to Real Estate teaching. If I did, I wouldn't have been encouraged to write this book. Everything I learn and invest in; I bring back into my business and share with my team.

Not everyone can afford to invest heavily into coaching, masterminds, and mentors. I remember panicking when I first signed up for coaching because we were broke and the coaching cost $1,000 a month. Sometimes it's also hard to get your spouse to support the decision to invest because it is so expensive and they don't necessarily understand the benefits. You have to be willing to make that commitment—and then *be committed*. You get out of it what you put into it!

There is a misconception that coaching and accountability always have to come at an expense. One of my first coaches, Kimberly Ryan, was a friend I trusted, and when I sought her guidance, she gave it for free. She was the best coach and mentor during the time shortly after my dad died. I was struggling in my business and personal life. When he passed, I assumed the leadership role, making sure everything was running smoothly with his business, employees and our family needs. I didn't take the time to grieve because I chose to step in and make sure things kept moving. Kim was instrumental in keeping me in alignment through all of the emotional experiences I was having.

She took me through an amazingly impactful exercise-one I love leading my coaching clients through as well. It's called the "Red Shirt" exercise. First, she asked me to write down every task I was doing in my business, from setting appointments to making calls. Then she asked, "If you were to hire someone, what jobs would you want to keep for yourself and what would you rather delegate?"

Eventually, she brought me to this question: "When you think about the legacy you want to create, what's the one word that describes you and where you want to be?"

That was years ago, before I knew I'd one day become a coach and influencer in the real estate industry. That one word described who I wanted to be, and it's still the essence of what I do today. I still have the big Post-it Note from that exercise where I wrote down that one, all-important word: *wealth-builder*. Whether someone is buying their first home, selling a house, or buying investment properties, I help people build wealth for now and for generations to come. Kim helped me understand the heart of what drives me, and I continue to build my entire career on the foundation of that passion.

Kim knew my heart, my family, and my business, and that made it easier for her to guide me into a better space. She cost me nothing and gifted me so much, personally and professionally. If funds are tight, look to your sphere for possible coaches or mentors who can help you and invest your time and effort just as you would if you were paying for their guidance.

In real estate, you can often be coached or mentored for free when you start out—many companies have mentorship programs. When I joined the family business with my parents, I worked for less money so I could be coached and mentored by a genius in the industry—Dad. Be willing to work for less, or even offer to help someone for free in the industry that you look up to, just to be around their influence and knowledge. Be willing to give up your time to play in the space of someone who's incredible in this business.

Traditionally we are willing to take out loans to go to college or trade school to be taught the basics in a field or profession. After you pay for that education, you then go out into the real world and have to acquire skills and experience before you can make the top dollar in that career.

Sometimes we pay for an internship or work for free to get that experience. For some reason in our industry people feel that once they pay for their minimal schooling and pass a test, they are now experts and entitled to big commissions. Real Estate is one of the few industries that has no ceiling. You have limitless opportunities and potential to earn and accumulate as much wealth as your imagination can muster up. Why then are we not willing to take a lower split or a small salary to learn from a master in our profession?

Listen: there's time, and there's money. If you don't have any money, you probably have time. If you invest that time to help yourself or someone else, they're going to invest in you as well. Take less money, find a mentor who is willing to invest their time in you so that you can be amazing and pay it forward!

Does it have to be a mentor or a coach? NO! You can spend as little as $100 a month for online or group coaching, or you can put together your own group of like-minded people to mastermind with. When the market went sideways in 2008, I got together with six or eight guys for coffee every Thursday morning at the local coffee shop just so we could share what was working/not working and talk about the market. That group forged some incredible lifelong friendships and industry partners. Anybody has the ability to do that.

When I first started in real estate, it was a non-sharing industry. Everybody was secretive about their strategies. Thankfully, that has changed. Put yourself out there and find a group to meet with on a regular basis. You can talk about the industry and personal stuff, too—an informal

INVEST IN YOURSELF

setting is great for finding support in all areas of your life, like challenges with childcare, work-life balance, etc. You can do this without spending money.

A word of advice though: Don't make it over cocktails, make it over coffee. I have some deep regrets from past masterminds because I can't remember the conversations, I had with some of the most influential people who've come into my life. I still remember sitting on the patio in my LA hotel one morning, writing in my journal—almost shaming myself, because I'd had the undivided attention from a billionaire sitting across the table from me the night before, and I couldn't remember what the guy said to me. I was too many cocktails in to really absorb everything I could have learned. If you want to go to happy hour, go for fun. If you want to truly connect and have a meaningful conversation, keep the sauce out of it.

If you do have a coach or mentor, I would also encourage you to set aside fifteen or twenty minutes before and after each call to really think about what you want to talk about and what actions you're going to take after the call. Don't show up to the call when you're in between appointments. Too many people, me included, have paid for things that you wind up doing absentmindedly when you're busy, rather than being intentional about it. That's like paying for a car you don't drive.

So how do you know when it's time to invest in a coach, mentor, or brain trust? The answer's simple: whenever you either feel stuck or you're ready to go to the next level.

Take stock of your life right now. Not just in your business, in your personal life, too. How's your health? What's holding you back? Is it your lack of energy? Your finances? Business systems? Your home life or marriage? Maybe your business is doing okay right now but would go through the roof if you got your health under control. If that's the piece that's holding you back, hire a personal trainer to get you fit and healthy again.

Maybe you just need coaching on time management or how to set up better systems or make better sales calls. Everything you learn levels up your business and productivity. A good coach can help you see things you are blind to. Sometimes you may need to work on an area in your life that you didn't even realize affects your business.

Maybe it's not coaching you need but more knowledge. What classes can you take to fill gaps in your skills? Learning levels up your business and your productivity. If you need help to nail down what you need, a coach can help you figure out what's a distraction versus what's truly important to where you are right now.

People ask me all the time how I create my lending sources. My response is always the same. "There are five people in your sphere who have money and would be willing to lend it to you if you have that conversation." But do you know how many people actually, follow through and have that conversation? In my experience, zilch. When I first started coaching, I felt like I was failing because I was trying to take responsibility for my clients' success. The reality is, your success isn't anyone else's responsibility. It's yours. The amazing thing is that if you do take the steps, you'll be excited about what you are able to achieve.

Be coachable. My dad was so set in his ways, he never would have been a good candidate for coaching. Being coachable means that you're flexible and open to new ideas. It means you're willing to shift if someone shows you a different way of doing things. Don't be scared to try new things you hadn't thought of.

Give that new thing a try for a full ninety days. If I told you that in order to increase your business you need to make five calls a day, you can't do that for a week and expect to see results. Similarly, you can't go out and hike for a week and eat well and expect to see things change on the scale. If you do those same things consistently for ninety days and then come back to the scale, you'll see a big change. When someone coaches you, jump in and try their suggestions for three full months.

Be willing to fail. You don't learn anything when things are easy. When you try new things, sometimes you'll fail. There's no better way to learn.

Like any investment, you need to do your due diligence before you decide who to work with. There's so much available, especially within the influencer world, and so many services you can buy into. Choosing the right option comes down to what you need. To get started, assess where you are right now, and where you'd like to go. Are you looking for self-improvement? Or are you looking for specific results with accountability to get you there? Are you looking for support in your personal life, or do you want someone who can help you restructure the backend operations of your business? As your career evolves, your needs will change, and you may look for coaching, mentorship, or a brain trust to serve different areas of your life and business as those needs change.

Ask yourself what you're willing to invest in this year. If you don't have $10,000 to invest in a private coach, then invest your time in someone who can teach you in exchange for your help. Nothing is out of your reach.

As you start to look for the right fit for you, here my top three considerations:

1. **Don't be afraid to look outside your industry.** Learning practices from other industries can give you that outside- the-box inspiration to advance to the next level of your own profession. Go explore! Go be an outsider and meet people who can give you a new perspective.

2. **Is it money you have more of, or time?** If you don't have the money to hire a coach or join a mastermind, consider creating your own tribe of like-minded people that can meet over coffee or lunch. You can create an accountability group on your own.

3. **Do your research and ask for referrals.** This is especially useful in finding a mentor who fits with your goals and making the most out of the time invested together. Ask for recommendations from your social media community or someone you know who's been coached and had success.

Chapter 10
Limitless Real Estate Strategies
The 10 Best Strategies of a Problem Solver

This is what you have been waiting for!!

Inside this chapter are all the strategies you can put into play as you move forward in growing your business—detailed here in order from the simplest to the most complicated. Once you understand these strategies, not only are you going to 2X, 3X, or 10X your income, you are going to build your own wealth. You're also going to be able to guide other people through the same process, because you've done it yourself. The best way to learn something and gain the expertise to teach others, *is to do it.*

We are playing chess, not checkers! Take your time and make calculated moves. Adopt these ten strategies into your business, and you will unlock all the power of your real estate license.

Strategy #1: Buy a house...and keep it!

The first step for you and your clients in your investment journey is to buy a house—with the mindset that you're buying your first rental property. Your first house won't be your forever home, although you are going to keep it forever. Mindset is key here. Maybe you'd like to buy a bigger, nicer home, but you're going to sacrifice instant gratification for long-term wealth.

I regret selling the first home I ever owned. I was 24. I'm not even sure where that money went. Had I kept that house through the changing markets, it would have been paid off by now and tripled in value. What I should have done was pull equity from the property, tax-free, and invested into another property rather than selling. Don't sell your homes. Use the equity to reinvest.

> Two years ago, Chris and Sheri decided to sell a rental house my dad sold to them twelve years ago. They purchased the house for $100,000. They had paid cash for it, and over the ten years they owned it as a rental property, the house appreciated to $300,000 in value. They called me and said, "Hey, we're done renting this house. We want to sell it so we can send our kids to school."
>
> I tried to talk them out of it. "Why not pull the equity to fund their kids' education," I suggested, "and keep renting the house?" They refused, and here's what happened. They sold the house for $280,000, from which they paid the cost of sale. They also had ten years of depreciation on the property, which they had to recapture at sale. By the time they factored in the tax consequence and the cost of sale, they profited only $130,000. That paid for their children's education.

Had Chris & Sheri kept the house, it would have gained another $100,000 by the height of the market in 2021. They could have pulled the money out by refinancing, the house would have continued to have a positive cash flow from rental income, been a tax write-off, and continued to appreciate. They would still own the real estate, they would still be getting money in their mailbox every month, the tenant would still be paying for it and the kids would still have gone to college without student loans! Everybody Wins!!!

Chris and Sheri were so focused on "debt-free" they lost sight of what their real estate could do for them. Despite the recent rise in interest rates, a mortgage is the cheapest debt you can borrow in the world.

That takes us to....

Strategy #2: Use dead equity to create your dream.

The reality is, your home's equity is money that's just sitting there, tied up and not making a return, when it could be used to grow your wealth. Talk radio and financial gurus of the world perpetuate the myth that you should work really hard to pay off your mortgage as quickly as possible. This is a good strategy for people who have limited income potential, are going to retire with a pension, or work for a company with outstanding benefits. Also, for people who will need to depend on equity late in life or don't have a retirement plan. When you are in an industry where the sky's the limit in the potential you have to earn money and find amazing investment opportunities...we use our equity!

Here's the crazy thing: You can move money from your primary residence, which is still a tax write-off, and put it into other properties—one or many. Now, you have rental income paying down that debt. Yes, most people are more comfortable when they don't have any debt. But truthfully, a debt-free house means you have a huge amount of dead equity just sitting there, doing nothing.

By refinancing or creating an equity line on your primary residence, you can use that otherwise "dead" equity to fund your next investment property. This strategy is accessible to anybody who owns a home.

Let's do a world problem:

You come to me for a strategy session to build your long-term plan based on your vision of the financial future you want to achieve in your lifetime. You owe $250,000 on your home. It is now worth $700,000. This means you have $450,000 in dead equity in your primary residence. Depending on your current interest rate I would advise you to either do a cash out refinance or a home equity line of credit (HELOC). With either product you need to leave 20% of the equity in the home. (On an investment property a HELOC is not allowed. You would have to refinance and the customary equity left in an investment property is 25%.) Here's the equation:

$450,000 (equity) x .80 (% you can pull out) = $360,000

You now have $360,000 to invest in rental properties. The cost of the payment on this money is about $2200 per month.

Here's an example of how you can put this equity to work. With that $360,000 from your primary residence. You can buy three $300,000 houses; putting $120,000 down on each and leveraging the other $180,000. Your payment for each new loan is about $1,150 principal and interest. Your HELOC payment is now divided among the three new properties at $735 each. Your financing is now costing $1885 per property.

The houses will likely rent for $2000 a month. Which means your cash flow is about $115 a month for each house.

This will likely cover property management and insurance, maybe slightly negative monthly, but let's take a look at what we have accomplished…

You now own $1.6M in Real Estate instead of $700,000 and you still have $495,000 in equity across all three properties!

Plus, you have the tax advantages of depreciation of the rental property. In five years, you could refinance a property, pull the equity out, and pay off the line of credit.

Now, here's the expert investor advantage. With the average market appreciation, you now have 4 houses appreciating at 6% annually. That's $96,000 in annual appreciation (market value) among the 4 properties. This comes into play when it's time to refinance and cash out on your new equity. These funds can now be used to purchase more properties or pay off the HELOC on your primary residence.

Of course, these numbers can vary depending on market conditions, rent in your area, interest rates and a variety of other factors. Your money is growing exponentially faster than when it was sitting as dead equity in your home. I think you can see the power of leveraging your dead equity.

Similarly, you can use your home's equity to fund your child's college education, as we talked about earlier. I can refinance and keep pulling cash out of properties with zero tax consequences for as long as I own them and they're still generating income.

A common strategy from financial influencers is to devote all your resources toward paying off your mortgage so instead of making mortgage payments, you invest that money into mutual funds hoping for a good rate of return. But you can grow your wealth much faster if you use your otherwise dead equity to invest in more real estate. Your money now works for you, bringing in rental income that pays for the cost of ownership. Plus, positive cash flow according to your long- term financial strategy. Eventually, your real estate portfolio will put positive cash flow into the monthly income goals you set when you created your wealth-building plan. You will have built a legacy portfolio to pass down to your children and grandchildren.

Strategy #3: Now that you're prepared for the opportunity, don't buy just to buy.

Throughout the book, we've talked about being prepared to capture opportunities when they come up, and how to develop situational awareness so you can find great properties that fit your Buy Box. I've given you the mindset you need to shift from a traditional agent into a problem solver and shown you how to use your knowledge and skills to create legacy and build wealth.

Remember, these are skills that you can build over time. You have the knowledge and mindset to build the kind of legacy I have built. When it comes to putting everything into practice, there's still a learning curve. That's okay. After you read this book, the next time a client comes to you and says, "Hey, my mom passed away and left me her home, and I don't know what to do with it. Can you help me?" you now have the mindset to see that as an opportunity and size it up against your bigger plan. Don't jump on every property you see, but wait for the right opportunity. Even if you buy a house this year at a price that seems a little high, keep on that same path—buy one property a year, or every two years. If you buy fifteen houses over your career, what would that change for your retirement, for your family, for your children?

Strategy #4: Flipping and wholesaling.

Flipping is a bit of a buzzword in that it's often talked about as one of the "easiest" ways to make money from real estate. This is not something everyone wants to do. If you own enough houses, you eventually learn how to flip them and make a profit. Flipping doesn't always come with a massive renovation or even a lot of repairs.

A good flipping process and workflow does take time to build. In order to buy and sell effectively and efficiently enough to make a good profit, it takes buying a good deal, even then it is not for the faint of heart, there is a lot of risk involved. Before you decide to flip check in with yourself on these things:

- Did I get a good deal and buy well?
- Know your audience, will this sell well? Don't over-improve or under-improve the property. Know the area and what other properties are selling for and what amenities they offer.
- Time is Money! Make sure you have your team in place and know your numbers before you start. That property costs money every day it sits vacant, know how much.
- What if? What is your exit plan if the rainbow and butterfly version doesn't work out.

Wholesaling is another buzzword in our industry. Rarely do people really understand what wholesaling and flipping actually involve, and they might not know whether they are missing out on bigger opportunities when they limit their focus on these two strategies.

Wholesaling is a way to make money without any money, which is why it appeals as an income stream. It's not for everyone, but it's a good niche for agents who are particularly adept at finding discount properties. Agents who wholesale negotiate a sale under contract with the seller, and then find an investor to buy the contract at a higher price than what they promised to the seller. They collect the difference as a fee. I worked with a wholesale agent for about two years. He would find the deals, I'd buy them, and he'd make about $5,000 per house.

In one year, his income totaled about $100,000. I made more than a million dollars by *buying* the properties. This is where mindset comes into play. If you're already good at turning over rocks to find screaming deals, imagine how much better off you'll be if you know how to capture those assets for yourself. If you're not adept at finding deals (or would rather hire out that task), consider working with a wholesaler to find properties for you.

The concepts of flipping and wholesaling are easy. What's hard is understanding how the numbers play out and knowing how to recognize a good deal. Does it fit into your long-term plan? Do you have the resources to renovate or repair houses that need improvement? You need to determine whether the strategies are right for you and whether the risks are worth the reward.

I don't flip houses for clients. When a client wants to buy a house as a rental property, we accommodate in one of two ways. I will find a house, assist them in purchasing it, and refer to my contractor to bring the house to a rent-ready state. The other way we will accommodate the investor is to buy the house at under market value, renovate the house, and then sell it to them. This is much like flipping, the only difference is they choose the house prior to renovation and because I have tied it up. They have time to get traditional financing and can include the cost of the repairs in the purchase price because it will appraise higher in renovated condition.

I won't manage the renovation on my client's behalf. Investor clients often have a mindset that their agent will do all the work for them, and agents put themselves in harm's way by taking on jobs they shouldn't just to secure the commission. Don't put yourself in harm's way. Chase the money, not the buyer.

Strategy #5: Money is everything.

I started to get really creative in understanding how the lenders worked and how to time my purchases. I realized that if I can buy the down payment in one house—meaning buying a home at 20%-30% discount—I was actually buying my down payment in the property using the equity. Rental income will cover all or most of my debt costs as long as I own that house. I started to focus on having really good conversations with people and learned how to ask the right questions to find more properties that I could buy at a discount.

Without spending a pile of money, time, and effort, I could solve problems for people *and* create opportunities for myself *at the same time*. The deeper the discount I could find, the more equity I created as the down payment. This strategy is actually a little different from the BRRR method of buy, renovate, refinance, repeat.

Think of it this way. The average agent makes around $75,000 to $100,000 a year. If you have to put down $40,000 to $80,000, depending on your market, it's going to take a while to save for that down payment. But if you can buy a property $40,000 to $80,000 below market, you just created your down payment for your next investment property. As long as you follow what lenders call the "Seasoning Policy," you can buy a house, then refinance it at 75%-80% loan- to-value using the equity as the down payment. According to the Seasoning Policy, lenders stipulate that you have to own a home for six to twelve months in order for them to use its appraised value to determine the equity you have as the down payment for that home. This is how you create equity and down payment from thin air.

What about your cash flow? I bought Jim's house in Chapter 2 for $102,500, and my monthly payment was about $1,600 in hard money. I rented the house for $1,300 a month, which meant I was in the negative $300 a month. I realized that if I could afford $3,600 a year—which is obviously much easier than trying to save the down payment for this property—I was basically buying the down payment for this property for just $300 a month.

At the end of that first year, the house appraised for $175,000. I refinanced the hard money loan into a mortgage with a traditional lender, paid back my mentor plus his promised interest, and used the equity (based on the appraised value) to refinance this house and the only money out of pocket was for the negative $300 a month while I waited to refinance.

This is my standard method of operating when it comes to purchasing rental homes. In order to be prepared to capture opportunity, you have to have good money relationships. Now that we have the down payment figured out, here are three key ways that create money relationships:

1. Hard Money Loans

Hard money is Private capital, secured by a deed similar to traditional lending. It usually comes at a higher interest rate and is borrowed for a short amount of time. Hard money is a way to leverage an asset based on the value you purchased it for. The interest rates are extremely high—typically 10%-15%, (sometimes more depending on credit, current rates and amount you are borrowing) In addition, to secure the loan you may have to put down 10%-20%, depending on the lender. This is a way for you to capture opportunities that you otherwise would have to pass up. For the lender, this is a way to invest and earn interest from their money. Hard money lenders may be someone you do or do not have a relationship with.

2. Relationship Capital

If we understand how money moves and breathes and what excites an investor, we can create relationship capital inside our sphere of influence. When you teach people to understand that you provide them with an opportunity to create monthly income with their uninvested or underinvested resources that are sitting stagnant. This is a way to raise enough capital to always be prepared to buy rentals or flips.

Here is an example: You and your client are having a conversation, and you ask them what rate of return they get on the stock market. They tell you between 7% and 10%. Ask them, "What happens if that mutual loses X amount of money? What happens to your retirement? What if I can give you a guaranteed, secured rate of return?"

When you invest in the stock market, there's no security. Your money is not secured by a tangible asset, it's not attached to a building, it's not attached to anything. It's just money in a fund that you hope earns you a return. But that return can also go to zero at any time. When you teach people how to invest their money into your projects, they're getting a guaranteed rate of return because it's secured by real estate. As the lender and lien holder, they get predetermined interest rate. With the property as collateral, they could also end up with the property if the loan defaults or they love the renovations so much, they want it for themselves. This is a win-win for everyone and a great option when you don't have cash for a down payment but you have found a sweet deal!

To tap into relationship capital, there are two parts to drawing up the legal agreement: a note and deed of trust. The note is the terms of the agreement. For example, say your investor is going to loan you $250,000 to buy 123 Main Street. That

$250,000 goes to the title company, and the title company secures a deed of trust against the property, which basically means your investor becomes the bank. You own the property; the property is deeded to you. Your investor has no liability for the property—not for taxes, insurance, or anything else. You are liable to your investor to make payments according to the terms of the agreement, for a specified period of time. The deed of trust is what ensures the investor receives funds when the property is sold or refinanced.

As an agent, you can view your investor clients in two ways: one of which is "I'm going to help you buy properties." The other is "You can invest your money with me; I'll buy the properties for my portfolio, and you'll earn interest on your money, secure and guaranteed." In order to create relationship capital, you have to be able to really create that trust between you and your investors. This is where I've been extremely successful with my clients and so can you.

I have some clients in their sixties, and they don't want to own properties at this stage in their lives. But they have cash! That's when I convert them from a rental investor to a cash lender. Relationship capital is really about building relationships with people who have money and then guide them to invest that money into your preparedness for opportunity. When I talk to people about money, I'm trying to get them to commit that they will lend me money if I find the right opportunity. My dad had a list of people he could have built relationship capital with. He only ever sold them houses; he never created the capital he needed to buy the houses himself. He would sell an opportunity to somebody and make $5,000, and they would make $50,000. Start building your relationship capital now. This is how you become limitless in real estate.

Your relationships with money also tie back to everything we talked about in the previous chapter because every time you participate in something like a mastermind or coaching program, you broaden your sphere of influence with people who are already in the mindset of using creative ways to invest their money and build their wealth, just like you.

3. Traditional Financing

This includes mortgages with typical banks. It's harder to capture opportunity using traditional financing because the process of getting money isn't as fast; you have to go through the steps to qualify, make the downpayment, inspections, appraisals, market interest rates etc. It's yet another type of financing available to you while you grow your relationship capital. The key with traditional financing is to keep your credit rating high so you can maximize the amounts you can borrow and negotiate the best rates.

Strategy #6: Say yes and figure it out later.

In a distressed situation—for example, someone inherits a house they don't have time or money to pour into—you may see that there's an opportunity for you to make money. You just may not be sure exactly what that entails at first. Your strategy is to say yes and figure it out later. You might need to determine whether it's a good rental property or something you would flip, either as is or after renovations. Maybe the property fits your Buy Box so well that you're willing to take on a non-cash-flowing property with hard money in order to refinance it and put it into your rental portfolio. Your decisions will be determined by your own Buy Box and where you currently are financially. Do you need to create income? Can you hold off on income?

There will come a time when you are prepared and ready to act on the next opportunity. Don't be in a rush, and know what you want for the long term. Remember, after you say yes, I am always a click away from helping you figure it out. You are not alone.

Keep in mind that when you're an active real estate agent (check with your CPA or IRS tax code as to what IRS considers an active investor versus a passive investor in real estate), you have different tax capabilities and benefits available to you. You need to seek legal and tax advice to help you determine how to use those benefits to your advantage.

Strategy #7: Surround yourself with the right people.

When it comes to your accountant and attorney, who does your team consist of? Make sure you hire people with experience in real estate investing. Ask them if they understand the tax advantages available to an active real estate agent and whether they're experienced with passive income from real estate investing.

One of the lessons that I learned is not to look for the cheapest professionals. Be willing to invest in the best. Your business professionals should also have requirements for you to have a strong working relationship. My CPA does quarterly planning sessions with my team and I, she is always available to offer her professional opinion when I need it. When my clients do a four-week strategy session with me, I recommend they take their plan to their CPA to help them execute it in the best way and enlist a lawyer to help them set up an estate plan for the assets.

Most agents worry about the cost of hiring experts like a CPA, instead of seeing them as a valuable investment. My CPA is an investment in my business and my personal wealth, and I reap the benefits every year when she files my taxes. In tax savings alone, she saves me way more money than she costs me in professional fees.

Hiring a knowledgeable CPA well-versed in real estate tax laws is one of the best things you can do for your career, your personal financial health, and your investment portfolio. And your clients, too. Because everything you learn from your CPA, you can turn right back around and use that knowledge to help your clients.

Once you set up your plan, stick to it, no matter what the market is doing. The law of averages will even out the highs and lows. And remember that in the beginning, you may not bring in much cash flow—in fact, you may just cover most of your expenses or even have a small negative cash flow. But keep your mind on your vision for long-term wealth and stay true to your plan. Let the end goal drive you.

Over the years, I have watched people do a lot of misguided things, rather than surrounding themselves with the right people who could give the correct advice. Sometimes they know what is needed but are not willing to pay the higher dollar for the expertise. Yet behind any successful corporation is a team of attorneys and CPAs making sure the company is set up with the right systems in place for the most efficiency and biggest tax benefit. Your legal and financial advisers need to be chess players too; you have to see three steps forward because you're not just planning for now, you're planning for your future.

Strategy #8: Teach others to invest.

This is where you can grow another side of your business. Once you have mastered the investment strategies covered in this book, you can teach others how to invest.

Statistically, in the market I am in, the average family will stay in a home between five and seven years. What if you could help them create a legacy for themselves and their children, also grow your business by teaching them the benefit of moving every two to three years, and keep each property as a rental? You've created a repeat client and changed their lives profoundly. We have also witnessed the children of those clients coming back to invest the same way!

Put yourself in the shoes of a consumer who wants to invest in real estate. Most likely, they'll ask around for a referral to an agent who can help them find properties to buy, fully expecting the agent to guide them. What happens when the consumer calls the traditional real estate agent? Most of the time, the agent won't be knowledgeable enough to help their client develop a sound investment strategy. To them, this is simply another sale. Remember the statistic I shared with you early in the book? 95% of agents do not own rental properties, but 100% will sell someone a rental property, knowing *nothing* about it. That's what I hope to change.

When someone comes to me and says, "I have half a million dollars cash to invest," I start to ask questions. "What's the goal? Do you want to create passive income or build a legacy portfolio for your kids and grandkids?" If the goal is to generate income, I'll ask them, "How much do you want? Three thousand dollars a month, or ten thousand?"

A lot of times, clients will respond, "Wow, I didn't even know that kind of monthly income was an option!"

This is when I enroll them in my paid strategy planning sessions. These are mandatory for any client who wants to start their investment journey with my company. I help them build a plan tailored to their goals, and then we start to look for properties.

This will give them the skills and knowledge to invest wisely anywhere in the country, not just with me. They can build their portfolio—and have a different kind of conversation with their realtor. They'll know what questions to ask and have a vision they can share to help the agent they work with to better understand what they want to accomplish. I have a network of agents that I have mentored and coached around the country that I am able to refer this business out to with the confidence that the investor will be taken care of.

Bring strategy sessions into your business, too, and create yet another income stream. You can teach buyers how to approach investing in a whole new way and get paid for your time. Then you can help them go out and start buying properties and get paid for that, too. My philosophy is, I want my clients to have a solid understanding of what I show them, and I want them to develop a new mindset before we even start looking at houses.

I show my clients how to invest in long-term planning, not just how to buy real estate. By charging for this strategy session, I am ensuring my buyer that the money spent is a far greater investment in their future than the loss would be with no plan or an agent with no experience in investing.

Strategy #9: Get a deed of trust.

We touched on this strategy already as part of building relationship capital, but it's important to think of a deed of trust as a strategy in itself. I have a deed of trust program, which means clients can loan their funds, securely, without ownership in the property, and I take on the liability. My clients get a monthly mailbox check—most of my investors earn around 8%, so a $300,000 investment, for example, produces about $1,700 to $1,800 a month in cash flow, secured by real estate. Principle is returned when the asset is sold or re-financed. Essentially, they are the bank!

For tax purposes, the income is considered passive income, not earned income, so there is a tax consequence. We send clients a form 1099INT at the end of every year for whatever interest they earned. A deed of trust is both a pitch strategy for you to raise capital to buy properties and also a strategy for retirement income that you can offer to your money relationships as an alternative to buying property. In this way, you can extend your business to include clients who may never even buy a house from you. It's a win-win.

Eventually you will amass enough wealth that, someday, you will become the bank for someone else!

Strategy #10: Have a plan and a vision.

Now for the fun part. You get to dream. I want you to sit down with a journal or some paper and do these two things:

1. Draw up your dream life budget. Use the worksheet included in the book to help you.
2. Take that dream budget, go back to Chapter 5, and fill your tool box.
3. Create your Limitless Strategy for creating generational wealth.

When you think about retiring and about retirement income, at what age do you want to start collecting your income, and how much monthly income do you want to have? Don't set your sights too low. I recently had a coaching client who said to me, "I want to make six thousand dollars a month in passive income."

"Will that give you the life you want to live when you retire?" I asked. They thought about it for a second. "Well, no." On average, my coaching clients set goals of about $20,000 to $25,000 per month. Some people overshoot it as well. They'll decide to aim for a million dollars a year in passive income. I always make them think about whether they really need that kind of money or if they just pulled that number out of the air. Be realistic, but be generous, too. You have to work hard to reach your goals, so make the reward worth it.

When I did this exercise, I wanted to create $50,000 a month in passive income by the time I retired. To come up with that number, I broke everything down into percentages. Cars, additional investments, travel, living expenses, and charity. This clear vision keeps me moving forward toward my goals, helps me make good decisions along the way, and reminds me of the rewards waiting on the other side of the hard work it takes to put these strategies in action.

Wende and I make sure that in our monthly budget and our dream budget we always have room for charitable giving. We are full believers that "To whom much has been given, much is required." If you are not familiar with this quote, it can be found in Luke 12:48.... or from Uncle ben to Peter Parker in Spiderman.

This is my goal: to help you create a legacy. Think about the legacy your parents left for you. For me, there was no monetary legacy from my dad; he did leave me with a wealth of knowledge and opportunity. If I were to die at age sixty-three, like my dad, Wende, Christian, and Chase would inherit a portfolio worth tens of millions. In addition to that, my life insurance would pay off the mortgages on that entire portfolio. If they wanted to, Wende and the boys would be able to walk away and not work for the rest of their lives. We are working to leave a legacy to our children's children, with the intention that our portfolio will go on as a living family trust for generations to come. This will allow them to continue to invest, grow the money and help people for a long time to come. Our goal as a family is to make a difference!

The Dirty Little Secret! 1031 Exchange.

This is information that best comes from your accountant and attorney. There are books written about the 1031-exchange, and not just from the IRS. This is an amazing real estate tool, because of the sensitive nature and the number of rules, I will not be going into detail here. Know that it is one of the most powerful strategies for real estate investors to defer the tax on proceeds from selling properties. There are many ins and outs, as well as loopholes and rules. I have a story to illustrate the power of this strategy. This is not the only way to use it, this strategy creates multi-millionaires out of average investors!

> **When a flip goes wrong, keep it, rent it, and 1031 exchange it.**
>
> We did a flip in Sun City, Arizona, which is a retirement community. We got to the closing table and the buyer backed out, just as the market was shifting. I asked the property management company what it would look like if we kept the house for an additional eighteen months and put the house up on the rental market?
>
> Based on the numbers they provided, that's what we decided to do. By the time the lease ended, the house had appreciated about 30%. I decided to sell it and move all my profits, tax-free, into another property. I didn't want to hang on to a rental in a retirement community because renters tend to be seasonal. I also didn't want to lose $20,000 of my equity to capital gains taxes.

> Through a 1031 exchange, I sold the house, took the $100,000 profit and used it as a down payment on a property I can keep for the next ten years. Unless the laws change, I could also sell that house and make $200,000, and move that money into the next house.

1031 exchanges are a great example of tax strategies most people don't know about, but one I have benefited from greatly. In the first place, when you sell an investment property, you have to pay capital gains tax. Under the 1031 exchange tax law, if you invest the proceeds into another "like-kind" property, you can defer that tax, and then do it again, and again.

Like any tax strategy, you need the guidance of a CPA who is an expert in real estate taxes so you can maximize your tax savings and minimize tax consequences of every purchase and sale.

I hope your eyes are opened to the power your real estate license holds. To take the next step, I encourage you to book a strategy session with me to create your plan for personal wealth. Together, we'll walk through your risk tolerance, consider things like whether you have a good income and credit rating, how financially stable you feel, whether you currently own a home, and whether you want your properties to cash flow for you now, or in ten or twenty years (or more).

We'll look at all the tax advantages, identify your Buy Box, and explore the benefits and consequences of all the options available to you. Step by step, we'll craft your short- and long-term plans to achieve your goals for financial wealth and the legacy you want to leave behind.

I want you and everyone who reads this book to understand that what I teach should be shared. Pass this book on to a colleague, educate your clients, teach your team what I've taught you. Your license is a powerful gateway to opportunity. Don't keep it to yourself.

Here's What to Do Next

No matter where you are in your real estate career or investment journey, I can show you the way to get from where you are to where you want to be:

- The real estate business you desire to have
- The wealth you want to build
- The life you will love
- The legacy you will leave behind

Here's how I can help you take action right away:

1. Follow Me on Social Media

Let's connect! You can find me on Instagram and YouTube @SteveDValentine. You can also get my best tips delivered straight to your phone! Text "limitless" to 602-560-7027 for weekly inspirational Real Estate, Wealth, Life and Legacy texts.

2. Listen To the Real Estate Revolution Podcast

Limitless strategies for real estate, wealth, life and legacy. Each episode contains interviews of everyday people just

HERE'S WHAT TO DO NEXT

like you trying to create the strategy that works for them. Listen to the podcast at stevedvalentine.com/podcast.

3. Join The Limitless Circle

Join my inner circle of like-minded people just like you at Stevedvalentine.com/limitlesscircle. Here you will have access to monthly training and tons of value that only my inner circle receives each month all based on Real Estate, Wealth, Life and Legacy.

Use promo code **limitlessbook** for an instant discount on all courses offered directly through the website.

4. Limitless Strategies Agent to Investor Course

By reading this book, you have been invited to check out our Limitless Strategies Agent to Investor Course. This course gives you everything you need from mindset to practical and tactical investment solutions that you can add to your real estate business right now. Join the course at Stevedvalentine.com/training.

5. Private Coaching

If you want to dive in fast and deep, I do private coaching and mentoring for people in the real estate space who are ready to jump in with both feet and make things really happen. If you aren't afraid of the commitment, hard work and the investment, this is for you! This is a limited program; coaching clients are accepted by application only. To apply, visit Stevedvalentine.com/mentor.

6. Additional Support

If you are not an agent and are looking for a real estate agent who can guide you to and through any solution go to limitlessstrategies.io.

7. Looking to join a national brokerage or make a change?

Check out the advantages of joining me at Real Brokerage! www.SteveDValentine.com/joinreal. There are 8 plus ways you can generate income through your real estate career at Real Brokerage. I joined real as another form of investing and you can too. I will show you how.

Acknowledgments

I want to thank the Lord for giving me the word LIMITLESS! Philippians 4:13 I can do all things through Christ! This is our family word I now live and teach every day.

Wende Valentine, my generous and patient wife and amazing mother to our boys. Thank you for standing at my side and supporting me these last 24 years in all my dreams and passions in life no matter which squirrel I have been chasing. Thank you for your guidance and partnerships in the businesses we've built. Wende, you have always been my biggest supporter and the one person who has had relentless faith in me through better and worse. I love you, Babe!

Christian and Chase, my boys! Love you boys and thank you for your fierce support. You have believed in me day in and day out! You have challenged me as a parent, as a professional, and as a friend. Thank you for trusting me with your ideas and obstacles, and opinions. I am growing as a person each day because of you two. I have proudly watched as you have the same impact on your own spheres. I'm excited to watch you execute these principles in your lives, and I can't wait to see how you improve them!

My sidekicks and partners in crime Tami Maass and Erica Knipp for being by my side throughout the past decade. You have been a very important part of our family. Our business would not operate without each of you, which has allowed me to continue to make a larger impact on our industry and the world. With the two of you by my side, I know I am free to dream because together there is nothing we can't do. Tami, your wise counsel and the way you help me think through the "interesting" situations I get myself into is priceless! I cannot imagine being where I am without you to bounce my ideas off of and reign me in when I get ahead of myself. Thank you for always being patient and firm with me, even when I don't want to hear it. You are a true friend and confidant and I appreciate you more than you know. Erica, you are the person that allows me to go and do and create and make $hit happen. Thank you! The people I have trusted blindly throughout the years to do things the way I would do them have been very far and few between. You are that person and a natural at what you do. I am so proud to call you my partner. You take great care with our clients and make sure things are on track as I continue to grab things out of thin air and make things happen.

My mom, Debbie Valentine, for teaching me how to show my first house and the valuable mentorship in the real estate business early in my career. Thank you for supporting me in all my directional changes throughout the course of my career. We've seen and learned a lot together!

My late father, my hero, and mentor in the real estate space, Dan Valentine. This book is a direct result of the legacy he left me in knowledge. The knowledge has far outlearned and outgrown any legacy of money he could have left behind. He is loved and missed.

Kimberly Ryan, my coach, my mentor, and my dear friend who coached me through 2015 when I wanted to quit the business!

Chris Harder, my mentor, friend, and real estate client who accepted my application to his Elite Entrepreneur Master Mind seven years ago, when I knew I had more to offer but didn't know where to start. You led and encouraged me to write this book and have a greater impact on the world through my knowledge and my heart.

Each and every client who has ever trusted me to guide them through their real estate strategy over the past 24 years. I would not be where I am at today without the support and the raving fans you have all been!

About the Author

Steve D. Valentine is a highly regarded real estate expert and entrepreneur with a remarkable journey of success in the industry. After re-starting from rock bottom following the 2008 housing crash, he has built his own real estate portfolio worth over $50 million through hard work, perseverance, and a commitment to building strong relationships.

Steve's belief in the importance of relationships has been a driving force behind his success. He has a natural ability to connect people with the right talent and experience to achieve their goals, and his clients often credit him with helping them navigate complex real estate transactions with ease.

Despite his busy schedule, Steve prioritizes his personal life and enjoys spending time with his family, cars, and God's word. He is a proud father to two adult boys, Christian and Chase, and is 24 years married to Wende, a successful entrepreneur who runs her own construction and redesign company.

When he's not working, Steve enjoys all things automotive, traveling, reading, and staying active through pickleball and other outdoor activities. He is also an avid supporter of local charities and organizations that help those in need in his community.

Made in the USA
Monee, IL
29 May 2023

34491824R00085